180 Days of PRACTICE

GRADE
1

HANDS-ON
STEAM

| Science | Technology | Engineering | Arts | Mathematics |

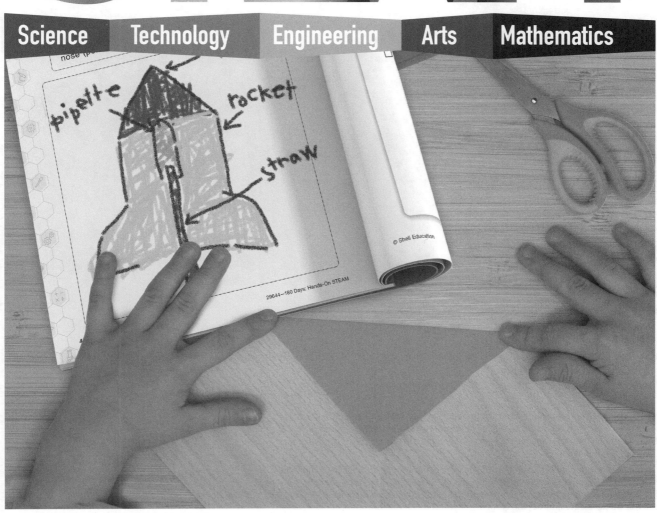

Kristi Sturgeon

Program Credits

Corinne Burton, M.A.Ed., *Publisher*
Emily R. Smith, M.A.Ed., *VP of Content Development*
Véronique Bos, *Creative Director*
Lynette Ordoñez, *Content Manager*
Melissa Laughlin, *Editor*
Jill Malcolm, *Graphic Designer*
David Slayton, *Assistant Editor*

Image Credits

All images from iStock and/or Shutterstock.

Standards

NGSS Lead States. 2013. *Next Generation Science Standards: For States, By States.* Washington, DC: The National Academies Press.
© 2021 TESOL International Association
© 2021 Board of Regents of the University of Wisconsin System

A division of Teacher Created Materials
5482 Argosy Avenue
Huntington Beach, CA 92649
www.tcmpub.com/shell-education
ISBN 978-1-4258-2528-7
© 2022 Shell Educational Publishing, Inc.
Printed in USA. WOR004

Table of Contents

Introduction

180 Days of Practice

Physical Science

Life Science

Earth and Space Science

Appendixes

Research

The Importance of STEAM Education

STEAM education is a powerful approach to learning that continues to gain momentum and support across the globe. STEAM is the integration of science, technology, engineering, the arts, and mathematics to design solutions for real-world problems. Students must learn how to question, explore, and analyze natural phenomena. With these skills in hand, students understand the complexity of available information and are empowered to become independent learners and problem solvers.

The content and practices of STEAM education are strong components of a balanced instructional approach, ensuring students are college- and career-ready. The application of STEAM practices in the classroom affords teachers opportunities to challenge students to apply new knowledge. Students of all ages can design and build structures, improve existing products, and test innovative solutions to real-world problems. STEAM instruction can be as simple as using recycled materials to design a habitat for caterpillars discovered on the playground and as challenging as designing a solution to provide clean water to developing countries. The possibilities are endless.

Blending arts principles with STEM disciplines prepares students to be problem solvers, creative collaborators, and thoughtful risk-takers. Even students who do not choose a career in a STEAM field will benefit because these skills can be translated into almost any career. Students who become STEAM proficient are prepared to answer complex questions, investigate global issues, and develop solutions for real-world challenges. Rodger W. Bybee (2013, 64) summarizes what is expected of students as they join the workforce:

> As literate adults, individuals should be competent to understand STEM-related global issues; recognize scientific from other nonscientific explanations; make reasonable arguments based on evidence; and, very important, fulfill their civic duties at the local, national, and global levels.

Likewise, STEAM helps students understand how concepts are connected as they gain proficiency in the Four Cs: creativity, collaboration, critical thinking, and communication.

Research *(cont.)*

Defining STEAM

STEAM is an integrated way of preparing students for the twenty-first century world. It places an emphasis on understanding science and mathematics while learning engineering skills. By including art, STEAM recognizes that the creative aspect of any project is integral to good design—whether designing an experiment or an object.

Science

Any project or advancement builds on prior science knowledge. Science focuses on learning and applying specific content, cross-cutting concepts, and scientific practices that are relevant to the topic or project.

Technology

This is what results from the application of scientific knowledge and engineering. It is something that is created to solve a problem or meet a need. Some people also include the *use* of technology in this category. That is, tools used by scientists and engineers to solve problems. In addition to computers and robots, technology can include nets used by marine biologists, anemometers used by meteorologists, computer software used by mathematicians, and so on.

Engineering

This is the application of scientific knowledge to meet a need, solve a problem, or address phenomena. For example, engineers design bridges to withstand huge loads. Engineering is also used to understand phenomena, such as in designing a way to test a hypothesis. When problems arise, such as those due to earthquakes or rising sea levels, engineering is required to design solutions to the problems. On a smaller scale, a homeowner might want to find a solution to their basement flooding.

Art

In this context, art equals creativity and creative problem-solving. For example, someone might want to test a hypothesis but be stumped as to how to set up the experiment. Perhaps you have a valuable painting. You think there is another valuable image below the first layer of paint on the canvas. You do not want to destroy the painting on top. A creative solution is needed. Art can also include a creative or beautiful design that solves a problem. For example, the Golden Gate Bridge is considered both an engineering marvel and a work of art.

Mathematics

This is the application of mathematics to real-world problems. Often, this includes data analysis—such as collecting data, graphing it, analyzing the data, and then communicating that analysis. It may also include taking mathematical measurements in the pursuit of an answer. The idea is not to learn new math, but rather to apply it; however, some mathematics may need to be learned to solve the specific problem. Isaac Newton, for example, is famous for *inventing* calculus to help him solve problems in understanding gravity and motion.

Research (cont.)

The Engineering Design Process

The most essential component of STEAM education is the engineering design process. This process is an articulated approach to problem solving in which students are guided through the iterative process of solving problems and refining solutions to achieve the best possible outcomes. There are many different versions of the engineering design process, but they all have the same basic structure and goals. As explained in Appendix I of NGSS (2013), "At any stage, a problem-solver can redefine the problem or generate new solutions to replace an idea that just isn't working out."

Each unit in this resource presents students with a design challenge in an authentic and engaging context. The practice pages guide and support students through the engineering design process to solve problems or fulfill needs.

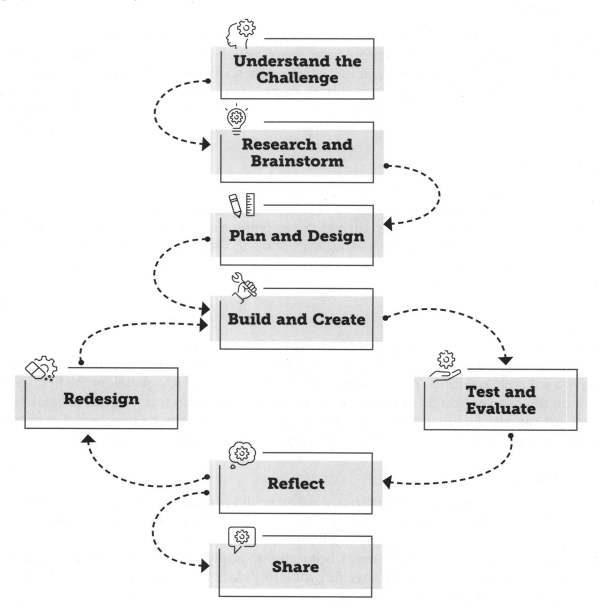

Research *(cont.)*

How to Facilitate Successful STEAM Challenges

There are some basic rules to remember as your students complete STEAM challenges.

Both independent and collaborative work should be included.

Astronaut and inventor Ellen Ochoa is well known for working a robotic arm in space. About that experience she said, "It's fun to work the robotic arm, in part because it's a team effort." She recognized that she was getting credit for something amazing that happened because of the collaborative work of hundreds of people.

Students need time to think through a project, both on their own and together with others. It is often best to encourage students to start by thinking independently. One student may think of a totally different solution than another student. Once they come together, students can merge aspects of each other's ideas to devise something even better.

Failure is a step in the process.

During the process of trying to invent a useful light bulb, Thomas Edison famously said, "I have not failed. I've just found 10,000 ways that won't work." People are innovating when they are failing because it is a chance to try something new. The STEAM challenges in this book intentionally give students chances to improve their designs. Students should feel free to innovate as much as possible, especially the first time around. Then, they can build on what they learned and try again.

Some students get stuck thinking there is one right way. There are almost always multiple solutions to a problem. For example, attaching train cars together used to be very dangerous. In the late nineteenth century, different solutions to this problem were invented in England and the United States to make the process safer. Both solutions worked, and both were used! Encourage students to recognize that there are usually different ways to solve problems. Discuss the pros and cons of the various solutions that students generate.

Research *(cont.)*

How to Facilitate Successful STEAM Challenges *(cont.)*

Getting inspiration from others is an option.

Students worry a lot about copying. It is important to remind them that all breakthroughs come on the shoulders of others. No one is working in a vacuum, and it is okay to get inspiration and ideas from others. It is also important to give credit to the people whose work and ideas inspired others. Students may see this as cheating, but they should be encouraged to see that they had a great enough idea that others recognized it and wanted to build on it.

The struggle is real—and really important.

Most people do not like to fail. And it can be frustrating not to know what to do or what to try next. Lonnie Johnson, engineer and toy inventor, advises, "Persevere. That's what I always say to people. There's no easy route." Try to support students during this struggle, as amazing innovations can emerge from the process. Further, students feel great when they surprise themselves with success after thinking they were not going to succeed.

Materials can inspire the process.

Students may be stumped about how they are going to build a boat…until you show them that they can use clay. A parachute is daunting, but a pile of tissue paper or plastic bags might suddenly make students feel like they have some direction. On the other hand, materials can also instantly send the mind in certain directions, without exploring other options. For this reason, consider carefully the point at which you want to show students the materials they can use. You might want them to brainstorm materials first. This might inspire you to offer materials you had not considered before.

Some students or groups will need different types of support.

If possible, have students who need additional support manipulate materials, play with commercial solutions, or watch videos to get ideas. For students who need an additional challenge, consider ways to make the challenge more "real world" by adding additional realistic criteria. Or, encourage students to add their own criteria.

How to Use This Resource

Unit Structure Overview

This resource is organized into 12 units. Each three-week unit is organized in a consistent format for ease of use.

Week 1: STEAM Content

Day 1 Learn Content	Students read text, study visuals, and answer multiple-choice questions.
Day 2 Learn Content	Students read text, study visuals, and answer short-answer questions.
Day 3 Explore Content	Students engage in hands-on activities, such as scientific investigations, mini building challenges, and drawing and labeling diagrams.
Day 4 Get Creative	Students use their creativity, imaginations, and artistic abilities in activities such as drawing, creating fun designs, and doing science-related crafts.
Day 5 Analyze Data	Students analyze and/or create charts, tables, maps, and graphs.

Week 2: STEAM Challenge

Day 1 Understand the Challenge	Students are introduced to the STEAM Challenge. They review the criteria and constraints for successful designs.
Day 2 Research and Brainstorm	Students conduct additional research, as needed, and brainstorm ideas for their designs.
Day 3 Plan and Design	Students plan and sketch their designs.
Day 4 Build and Create	Students use their materials to construct their designs.
Day 5 Test and Evaluate	Students conduct tests and/or evaluation to assess the effectiveness of their designs and how well they met the criteria of the challenge.

Week 3: STEAM Challenge Improvement

Day 1 Reflect	Students answer questions to reflect on their first designs and make plans for how to improve their designs.
Day 2 Redesign	Students sketch new or modified designs.
Day 3 Rebuild and Refine	Students rebuild or adjust their designs.
Day 4 Retest	Students retest and evaluate their new designs.
Day 5 Reflect and Share	Students reflect on their experiences working through the engineering design process. They discuss and share their process and results with others.

How to Use This Resource *(cont.)*

Pacing Options

This resource is flexibly designed and can be used in tandem with a core curriculum within a science, STEAM, or STEM block. It can also be used in makerspaces, after-school programs, summer school, or as enrichment activities at home. The following pacing options show suggestions for how to use this book.

Option 1

This option shows how each unit can be completed in 15 days. This option requires approximately 10–20 minutes a day. Building days are flexible, and teachers may allow for additional time at their discretion.

	Day 1	**Day 2**	**Day 3**	**Day 4**	**Day 5**
Week 1	Learn Content	Learn Content	Explore Content	Get Creative	Analyze Data
Week 2	Understand the Challenge	Research and Brainstorm	Plan and Design	Build and Create	Test and Evaluate
Week 3	Reflect	Redesign	Rebuild and Refine	Retest	Reflect and Share

Option 2

This option shows how each unit can be completed in fewer than 15 days. This option requires approximately 45–60 minutes a day.

	Day 1	**Day 2**
Week 1	Learn Content Explore Content	Get Creative Analyze Data
Week 2	Understand the Challenge Research and Brainstorm Plan and Design	Build and Create Test and Evaluate
Week 3	Reflect Redesign Rebuild and Refine	Retest Reflect and Share

How to Use This Resource *(cont.)*

Teaching Support Pages

Each unit in this resource begins with two teaching support pages that provide instructional guidance.

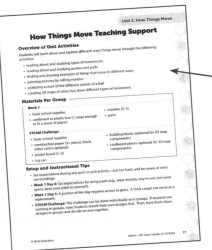

A clear overview of unit activities, weekly materials, safety notes, and setup tips help teachers plan and prepare efficiently and with ease.

Discussion questions help students verbalize their learning and connect it to their own lives.

Possible student misconceptions and design solutions help take the guesswork out of lesson planning.

Differentiation options offer ways to support and extend student learning.

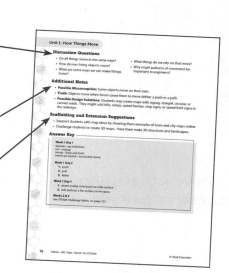

Materials

Due to the nature of engineering, the materials listed are often flexible. They may be substituted or added to, depending on what you have available. More material options require greater consideration by students and encourage more creative and critical thinking. Fewer material options can help narrow students' focus but may limit creativity. Adjust the materials provided to fit the needs of your students.

Approximate amounts of materials are included in each list. These amount suggestions are per group. Students are expected to have basic school supplies for each unit. These include paper, pencils, markers or crayons, glue, tape, and scissors.

How to Use This Resource *(cont.)*

Student Pages

Be sure to read aloud all text on student pages, and support comprehension as needed. You may also wish to have students verbally share answers with partners rather than write their answers. At this level, students may need additional support brainstorming or designing solutions for the STEAM Challenges. See the differentiation suggestions on the Teaching Support Pages for additional ways to support students.

Students begin each unit by learning about and exploring science-related content.

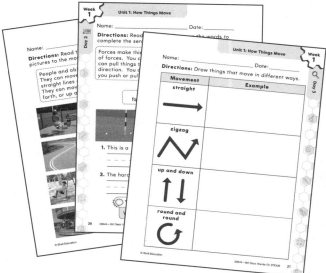

Activities in **Week 1** help build background science content knowledge relevant to the STEAM Challenge.

Creative activities encourage students to connect science and art.

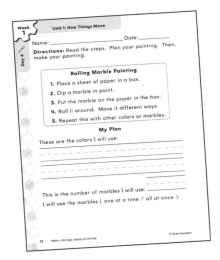

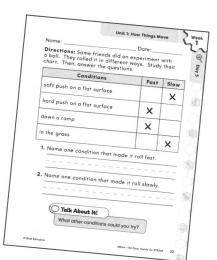

Graphs, charts, and maps guide students to make important mathematics and real-world connections.

How to Use This Resource (cont.)

Student Pages (cont.)

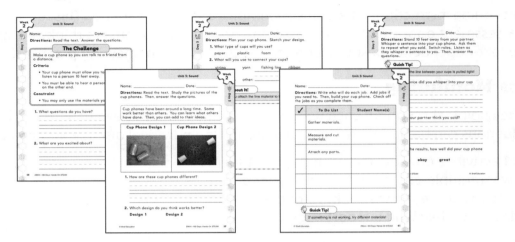

Week 2 introduces students to the STEAM Challenge. Activities guide students through each step of the engineering design process. They provide guiding questions and space for students to record their plans, progress, results, and thinking.

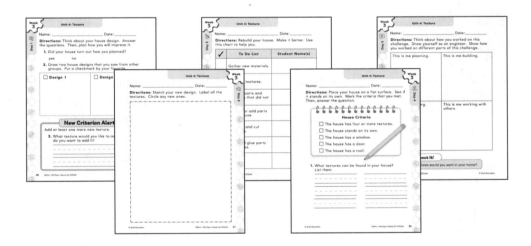

Week 3 activities continue to lead students through the cycle of the engineering design process. Students are encouraged to think about and discuss ways to improve their designs based on their observations and experiences in Week 2.

Quick Tip!

Staple all the student pages for each unit together, and distribute them as packets. This will allow students to easily refer to their learning as they complete the STEAM Challenges.

How to Use This Resource (cont.)

Assessment Options

Assessments guide instructional decisions and improve student learning. This resource offers balanced assessment opportunities. The assessments require students to think critically, respond to text-dependent questions, and utilize science and engineering practices.

Progress Monitoring

There are key points throughout each unit when valuable formative evaluations can be made. These evaluations can be based on group, paired, and/or individual discussions and activities.

- **Week 1** activities provide opportunities for students to answer multiple-choice and short-answer questions related to the content. Answer keys for these pages are provided in the Teaching Support pages.

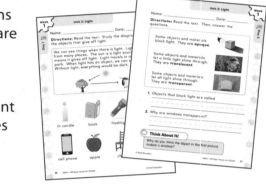

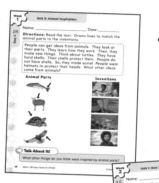

- **Talk About It!** graphics on student activity sheets offer opportunities to monitor student progress.

- **Week 2 Day 3: Plan and Design** is when students sketch their first designs. This is a great opportunity to assess how well students understand the STEAM challenge and what they plan to create. These should be reviewed before moving on to the Build and Create stages of the STEAM Challenges.

Summative Assessment

A rubric for the STEAM Challenges is provided on page 221. It is important to note that whether students' final designs were successful is not the main goal of this assessment. It is a way to assess students' skills as they work through the engineering design process. Students assess themselves first. Teachers can add notes to the assessment.

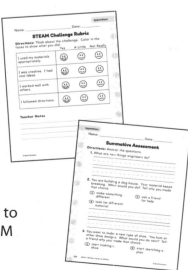

A short summative assessment is provided on page 222. This is meant to provide teachers with insight into how well students understand STEAM practices and the engineering design process.

© Shell Education

Standards Correlations

Shell Education is committed to producing educational materials that are research and standards based. To support this effort, this resource is correlated to the academic standards of all 50 states, the District of Columbia, the Department of Defense Dependent Schools, and the Canadian provinces. A correlation is also provided for key professional educational organizations.

To print a customized correlation report for your state, visit our website at **www.tcmpub.com/administrators/correlations** and follow the online directions. If you require assistance in printing correlation reports, please contact the Customer Service Department at 1-800-858-7339.

Standards Overview

The Every Student Succeeds Act (ESSA) mandates that all states adopt challenging academic standards that help students meet the goal of college and career readiness. While many states already adopted academic standards prior to ESSA, the act continues to hold states accountable for detailed and comprehensive standards. Standards are designed to focus instruction and guide adoption of curricula. They define the knowledge, skills, and content students should acquire at each level. Standards are also used to develop standardized tests to evaluate students' academic progress. State standards are used in the development of our resources, so educators can be assured they meet state academic requirements.

Next Generation Science Standards

This set of national standards aims to incorporate science knowledge and process standards into a cohesive framework. The standards listed on page 16 describe the science content and processes presented throughout the lessons.

TESOL and WIDA Standards

In this book, the following English language development standards are met: Standard 1: English language learners communicate for social and instructional purposes within the school setting. Standard 3: English language learners communicate information, ideas and concepts necessary for academic success in the content area of mathematics. Standard 4: English language learners communicate information, ideas and concepts necessary for academic success in the content area of science.

Standards Correlations (cont.)

Each unit in this resource supports the following NGSS Scientific and Engineering Practices and Engineering Performance Expectations for K–2.

Scientific and Engineering Practices	Engineering Performance Expectations
Asking Questions and Defining Problems	Ask questions, make observations, and gather information about a situation people want to change to define a simple problem that can be solved through the development of a new or improved object or tool.
Developing and Using Models	
Planning and Carrying Out Investigations	
Analyzing and Interpreting Data	Develop a simple sketch, drawing, or physical model to illustrate how the shape of an object helps it function as needed to solve a given problem.
Constructing Explanations and Designing Solutions	
Engaging in Argument from Evidence	Analyze data from tests of two objects designed to solve the same problem to compare the strengths and weaknesses of how each performs.
Obtaining, Evaluating, and Communicating Information	

This chart shows how the units in this resource align to NGSS Disciplinary Core Ideas and Crosscutting Concepts.

Unit	Disciplinary Core Idea	Crosscutting Concept
How Things Move	PS2.A: Forces and Motion	Cause and Effect
Light	PS4.B: Electromagnetic Radiation PS4.C: Information Technologies and Instrumentation	Cause and Effect
Sound	PS4.A: Wave Properties PS4.C: Information Technologies and Instrumentation	Cause and Effect
Texture	PS1.A: Structure and Properties of Matter	Patterns; Systems and System Models
Animal Inspiration	LS1.A: Structure and Function	Patterns; Structure and Function
Plant Inspiration	LS1.A: Structure and Function	Patterns; Structure and Function
Signs and Signals	LS1.B: Growth and Development of Organisms LS1.D: Information Processing	Patterns; Structure and Function
Traits	LS3.A: Inheritance of Traits LS3.B: Variation of Traits	Patterns
Conservation	ESS3.C: Human Impacts on Earth Systems	Systems and System Models
The Moon	ESS1.A: The Universe and its Stars	Patterns
The Seasons	ESS1.B: Earth and the Solar System	Patterns
The Stars	ESS1.A: The Universe and its Stars	Patterns

How Things Move Teaching Support

Overview of Unit Activities

Students will learn about and explore different ways things move through the following activities:

- reading about and studying types of movements
- reading about and studying pushes and pulls
- finding and drawing examples of things that move in different ways
- painting pictures by rolling marbles
- analyzing a chart of the different speeds of a ball
- creating 3D maps of cities that show different types of movement

Materials Per Group

Week 1

- basic school supplies
- cardboard or plastic box (1; large enough to fit a sheet of paper)
- marbles (3–5)
- paint

STEAM Challenge

- basic school supplies
- construction paper (5+ pieces; black, other colors optional)
- poster board (1–2)
- toy car
- building blocks (optional for 3D map components)
- cardboard pieces (optional for 3D map components)

Setup and Instructional Tips

- Set expectations during any push or pull activity—not too hard, and be aware of one's surroundings.
- **Week 1 Day 4:** Set expectations for using paint (e.g., wear smocks, stay in your personal space, keep your paint to yourself).
- **Week 1 Day 5:** A portion of this day requires access to grass. A thick carpet can serve as a replacement.
- **STEAM Challenge:** The challenge can be done individually or in groups. If students are working in groups, have students sketch their own designs first. Then, have them share designs in groups and decide on one together.

Discussion Questions

- Do all things move in the same ways?
- How do non-living objects move?
- What are some ways we can make things move?
- What things do we rely on that move?
- Why might patterns of movement be important to engineers?

Additional Notes

- **Possible Misconception:** Some objects move on their own.
- **Truth:** Objects move when forces cause them to move (either a push or a pull).
- **Possible Design Solutions:** Students may create maps with zigzag, straight, circular, or curved roads. They might add hills, ramps, speed bumps, stop signs, or speed limit signs in the redesign.

Scaffolding and Extension Suggestions

- Support students with map ideas by showing them examples of town and city maps online.
- Challenge students to create 3D maps. Have them make 3D structures and landscapes.

Answer Key

Week 1 Day 1
seesaw—up and down
car—zigzag
swing—back and forth
merry-go-round—round and round

Week 1 Day 2
1. push
2. pull
3. faster

Week 1 Day 5
1. down a ramp; hard push on a flat surface
2. soft push on a flat surface; in the grass

Weeks 2 & 3
See STEAM Challenge Rubric on page 221.

Name: _____ Date: _____

Directions: Read the text. Draw lines to match the pictures to the movements.

> People and objects can move in many ways. They can move in patterns. They can move in straight lines or curved lines. They can zigzag. They can move round and round, back and forth, or up and down.

zigzag

round and round

up and down

back and forth

Day 2

Name: _____ Date: _____

Directions: Read the text. Then, use the words to complete the sentences.

Forces make things move. Pushes and pulls are types of forces. You can push things away from you. You can pull things toward you. You can change their direction. You can change their speed. The harder you push or pull something, the faster it will go.

Word Bank

faster   pull   push

1. This is a
_____

— — — — — — — — — —

_____.

2. This is a
_____

— — — — — — — — — —

_____.

3. The harder you push something, the
_____

— — — — — — — — — — —

_____ it will go.

 Talk About It!

What are some things you push *and* pull?

Name: _____ Date: _____

Directions: Draw things that move in different ways.

Movement	Example
straight →	
zigzag	
up and down	
round and round	

Name: _____ Date: _____

Directions: Read the steps. Plan your painting. Then, make your painting.

> ### Rolling Marble Painting
>
> **1.** Place a sheet of paper in a box.
>
> **2.** Dip a marble in paint.
>
> **3.** Put the marble on the paper in the box.
>
> **4.** Roll it around. Move it different ways.
>
> **5.** Repeat this with other colors or marbles.

My Plan

These are the colors I will use:

_____

_____

_____

_____

_____

This is the number of marbles I will use: _____

I will use the marbles (one at a time / all at once).

Name: _____ Date: _____

Directions: Some friends did an experiment with a ball. They rolled it in different ways. Study their chart. Then, answer the questions.

Conditions	Fast	Slow
soft push on a flat surface		X
hard push on a flat surface	X	
down a ramp	X	
in the grass		X

1. Name one condition that made it roll fast.

_____

– –

_____

2. Name one condition that made it roll slowly.

_____

– –

_____

 Talk About It!

What other conditions could you try?

Name: _____ Date: _____

Directions: Read the text. Answer the question.

The Challenge

A town needs new roads. You are a city engineer. Create a town road map. Show different ways cars move through the town.

Criteria

- Cars must be able to move through the town in three or more ways (straight line, curved line, zigzag, round and round, back and forth, up and down, fast, or slow).
- The map must show at least four main places in the town.

Constraints

- You may only use the materials you are given.
- The town must fit on a sheet of poster board.

1. What questions do you have?

_____

_ _

_____

_ _

_____

Quick Tip!

Making cars go up and down on a flat map might be tricky. You could add a 3D hill or ramp.

Day 2

Name: _____ Date: _____

Directions: Write ideas for places in a town. Then, draw different roads.

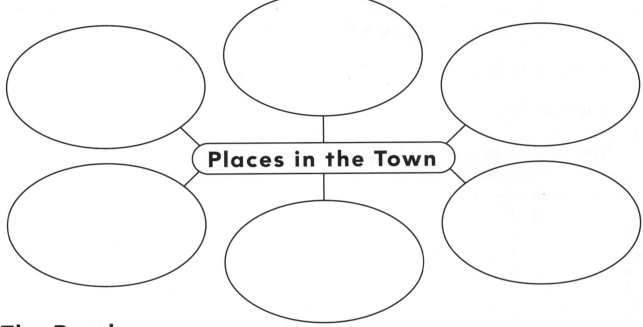

Places in the Town

The Roads

Draw a road where cars move in a straight line.	Draw a road where cars must zigzag.	Draw a road where cars can go round and round.

Name: _____ Date: _____

Directions: Sketch a town map. Label the ways cars will move. Label the places and buildings.

Types of Movement

back and forth	round and round	up and down
curved line	slow	zigzag
fast	straight line	

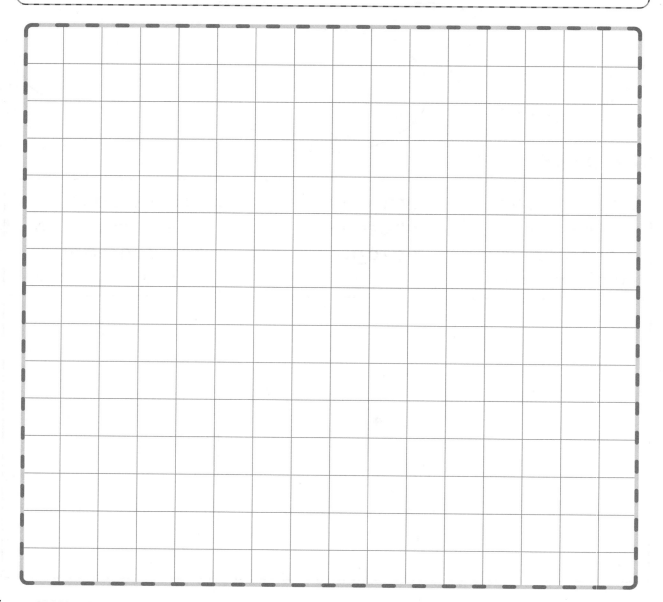

Name: _____ Date: _____

Directions: Write who will do each job. Add jobs if you need to. Then, create your map. Check off the jobs as you complete them.

✓	To Do List	Student Name(s)
	Gather materials.	
	Draw or cut and glue roads.	
	Draw or cut and glue places.	
	Color and label parts of the town.	
	Build and attach 3D parts (optional).	

 Quick Tip!

It is okay to change your design as you go!

Name: _____ Date: _____

Directions: Present your map to others. Plan what you will say. Then, tell them about it. Show them how cars move along the roads. Write what they say.

Tell

1. What three different ways can cars move through the town?

_____

_ _ _ _ _ _ _ _ _ _ _ _ _ _ _ _ _ _ _

_____

_____

_ _ _ _ _ _ _ _ _ _ _ _ _ _ _ _ _ _ _

_____

2. What main places did you show on your map?

_____   _____

_ _ _ _ _ _ _ _ _   _ _ _ _ _ _ _ _ _

_____   _____

_____   _____

_ _ _ _ _ _ _ _ _   _ _ _ _ _ _ _ _ _

_____   _____

Show

3. Model how the toy car moves through the town.

4. Does the toy car fit on all roads?   yes   no

Ask

5. How can I make it better?

_____

_ _ _ _ _ _ _ _ _ _ _ _ _ _ _ _ _ _ _

_____

Day 1

Name: _____ Date: _____

Directions: Think about the town map design. Answer the questions. Then, plan how you will improve it.

1. What part of the map do you like best?

_____

_ _

_____

2. What would you remove from the map, if anything?

_____

_ _

_____

3. What would you add to the map, if anything?

_____

_ _

_____

New Criterion Alert!

Add a fast zone and a slow zone to your map.

4. Where should the fast zone go?

_____

_ _ _ _ _ _ _ _ _ _ _ _ _ _ _ _ _ _ _

_____

5. Where should the slow zone go?

_____

_ _ _ _ _ _ _ _ _ _ _ _ _ _ _ _ _ _ _

_____

Unit 1: How Things Move

Name: _____ Date: _____

Directions: Sketch your new design. Write any new materials you will need.

New Materials

_____   _____   _____

- -

_____   _____   _____

_____   _____   _____

- -

_____   _____   _____

Name: _____ Date: _____

Directions: Rebuild the town map. Make it better.
Use this chart to help you.

 Quick Tip!

You do not have to start from scratch! You can make
changes to your first map.

✔	To Do List	Student Name(s)
	Gather new materials.	
	Add, remove, or change roads.	
	Add, remove, or change places.	
	Color your map.	
	Add or change 3D parts (optional).	
	Create a fast zone.	
	Create a slow zone.	

Name: _____ Date: _____

Directions: Present your new map to others. Plan what you will say. Then, tell them about it. Show them how cars move along the roads. Write what they say.

Tell

1. How did you improve the town map?

_____

- - - - - - - - - - - - - - - - - - - -

_____

- - - - - - - - - - - - - - - - - - - -

_____

2. Where did you put your fast and slow zones?

_____

- - - - - - - - - - - - - - - - - - - -

_____

- - - - - - - - - - - - - - - - - - - -

_____

Show

3. Model how the toy car moves through the town.

4. Model how it moves in the fast and slow zones.

Ask

5. How could I make it better next time?

_____

- - - - - - - - - - - - - - - - - - - -

_____

Name: _____ Date:_____

Directions: Think about how you worked on this challenge. Answer the questions.

1. What was your favorite part about creating a town map?

   _____

   _

   _____

   _

   _____

2. What name would you give the town you created? Write it in large, fun letters.

Talk About It!

Why would this town be a good place to live?

What other things might town planners and engineers have to think about?

Light Teaching Support

Overview of Unit Activities

Students will learn about and explore light sources and how light travels through the following activities:

- reading about and studying how light helps us see
- reading about and studying how light travels through materials
- experimenting with shining light on different materials
- making and tracing shadows in the sun and writing stories about them
- analyzing a chart showing how light travels through different materials
- creating secret codes with flashlights

Materials Per Group

Week 1

- basic school supplies
- chalk
- flashlight
- plastic wrap (1 sheet)
- tissue paper (1 sheet)
- wax paper (1 sheet)
- wood block or board

STEAM Challenge

- basic school supplies
- colored tissue paper (2–3 different colors, 1 sheet of each)
- flashlights (2)

Setup and Instructional Tips

- Set expectations for using flashlights (e.g., do not shine directly at someone's eyes).
- **STEAM Challenge:** This challenge is best done in partners, as it involves codes between two people. On testing days, be sure there is still enough light to write answers.
- **Week 2 Day 2:** Provide students with a few examples of codes (e.g., one flash, two flashes, light beam side to side, light beam up and down, light beam making a circle or other shapes, making finger shadows in front of the light onto a wall).

Discussion Questions

- Where does light come from?
- What human-made objects provide light?
- How would you describe objects that block light?
- How can we use light to solve problems?
- What are codes, and why do people use them?

Additional Notes

- **Possible Misconception:** Everyone has access to light.
- **Truth:** Everyone has access to natural light (the sun), but not everyone has access to electricity or batteries, both of which are needed to use human-made light sources.
- **Possible Design Solutions:** Students may create language codes using flashing light patterns, designs or patterns in shadows, or a combination of both.

Scaffolding and Extension Suggestions

- Support students with code ideas by practicing Morse code using flashlights. Give them copies of Morse code to use as starting points for their own codes.
- Challenge students to create codes for each letter in the alphabet, along with their words and questions.

Answer Key

Week 1 Day 1

The following items should be circled: lit candle, flashlight, cell phone, sun

Week 1 Day 2
1. opaque
2. Example: Windows are transparent so that people can see outside and let light in.

Week 1 Day 5
1. C
2. Both glasses have the same shape. The sunglasses block some light. The reading glasses do not.

Weeks 2 & 3

See STEAM Challenge Rubric on page 221.

Name: _____ Date: _____

Directions: Read the text. Study the diagram. Circle the objects that give off light.

We can see things when there is light. Light comes from many places. The sun is a light source. That means it gives off light. Light travels in a straight path. When light hits an object, we can see it. Without light, everything would be dark.

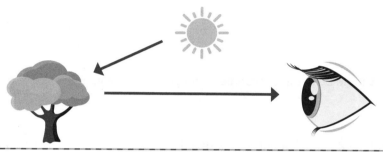

lit candle

book

flashlight

bike

cell phone

apple

chair

sun

Name: _____ Date: _____

Directions: Read the text. Then, answer the questions.

Some objects and materials block light. They are **opaque**.

Some objects and materials let a little light shine through. They are **translucent**.

Some objects and materials let all light shine through. They are **transparent**.

1. Objects that block light are called

_____

_ _

_____.

2. Why are windows transparent?

_____

_ _

_____

 Think About It!

Why do you think the object in the first picture makes a shadow?

Name: _____ Date: _____

Directions: Shine a flashlight at different things. Record your observations in the chart. Tell whether each one is opaque, translucent, or transparent.

Material or Object	Observations
wax paper	
wood	
plastic wrap	
tissue paper	

☆ **Try This!**

Think of other things you can test. Write them in the chart. Shine the light on them. Record your observations.

Name: _____ Date: _____

Directions: Create shadow art. Go outside with some chalk. Take turns tracing each other's shadows. Make a scene with your shadows. Draw what your scene looks like below. Then, write a story about what is happening in your scene. Share your story with others.

Shadow Scene

Shadow Scene Story

_____

- -

_____

- -

_____

- -

_____

Unit 2: Light

Name: _____ Date: _____

Directions: Study the chart. Answer the questions.

Transparent (*All* light shines through.)	**Translucent** (*Some* light shines through.)	**Opaque** (*No* light shines through.)

1. A pencil is _____.

    Ⓐ transparent   Ⓒ opaque

    Ⓑ translucent

2. Look at the two pairs of glasses. How are they similar? How are they different?

_____

_ _

_____

_ _

_____

Name: _____ Date: _____

Directions: Read the text. Answer the questions.

The Challenge

Design a code that uses light from a flashlight. Use it to send messages to a friend.

Criteria

- The code must use light to send messages.

- Your partner must be able to decode your messages.

Constraints

- You may only use the materials you are given.

- You must communicate without sound.

1. What are you wondering?

_____

_ _ _ _ _ _ _ _ _ _ _ _ _ _ _ _ _ _ _

_____

_____

_ _ _ _ _ _ _ _ _ _ _ _ _ _ _ _ _ _ _

_____

2. Write the challenge in your own words.

_____

_ _ _ _ _ _ _ _ _ _ _ _ _ _ _ _ _ _ _

_____

_____

_ _ _ _ _ _ _ _ _ _ _ _ _ _ _ _ _ _ _

_____

Name: _____ Date: _____

Directions: Brainstorm ideas for codes. Write them in the circles. For example, how could you use flashes of light? How could you use shadows?

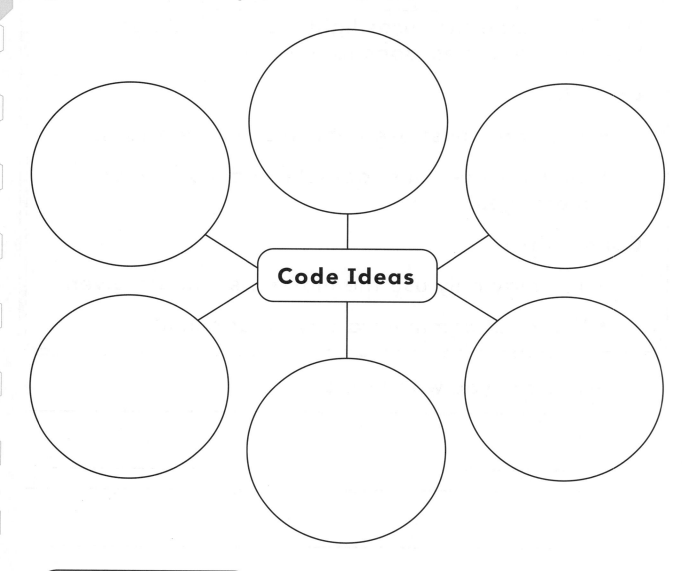

Code Ideas

☆ **Try This!**

Research what Morse code is. Think about how it could be used with light. How would you say *hello*?

Name: _____ Date: _____

Directions: Plan messages to send. List questions you may want to ask. Write the possible answers. Then, draw stars next to the ways your code will send messages.

Questions	Possible Answers
Example: Do you want a snack?	Example: Yes/No/Later

Ways My Code Will Send Messages

- turning the flashlight on and off

- waving my hand over the light

- moving the flashlight in different directions

- making shapes by moving the flashlight

- making shadows with my hand

_____

- my idea: _____

Week 2

Day 4

Name: _____ Date: _____

Directions: Read the example code plans. Then, work with a partner to write your code. Write words and questions you want in your code. Explain what the code will be for each one.

Example Code

Word or Question	Flashlight Code
Do you want a snack?	shadow of hand moving like mouth
Yes	two quick flashes on and off

My Code

Word or Question	Flashlight Code

Name: _____ Date: _____

Directions: Find a dark place to test your code. Sit five or more feet (1.5 m) from your partner. Take turns using your code to ask questions. Write your questions. Write your partner's answers. Then, answer the question.

Question I Asked	My Partner's Answer

1. Did you understand your partner's questions?

yes   **no**

Unit 2: Light

Name: _____ Date: _____

Directions: Think about your flashlight code. Answer the questions.

1. Was it easier to send or receive a message? Why?

_____

- - - - - - - - - - - - - - - - - - - -

_____

_____

- - - - - - - - - - - - - - - - - - - -

_____

2. What worked well with your flashlight code?

_____

- - - - - - - - - - - - - - - - - - - -

_____

3. What do you want to change or add to your flashlight code?

_____

- - - - - - - - - - - - - - - - - - - -

_____

New Material Alert!

You may now use colored tissue paper if you want. How could you use the colored tissue paper to communicate?

_____

- - - - - - - - - - - - - - - - - - - -

_____

_____

- - - - - - - - - - - - - - - - - - - -

_____

Name: _____ Date: _____

Directions: Plan messages you will send with your new code. List questions you may want to ask. Write possible answers. Draw a star next to questions that are new. Then, draw stars next to the ways your new code will send messages.

Questions	Possible Answers
Example: Do you want a snack?	Example: Yes/No/Later

Ways My New Code Will Send Messages

- turning the flashlight on and off

- waving my hand over the light

- moving the flashlight in different directions

- making shapes by moving the flashlight

- making shadows with my hand

- placing different colors of tissue paper in front of the light

- my idea: _____

Name: _____ Date: _____

Directions: Rewrite your code. Write words and questions you want in your code. Write what the code will be for each one.

My New Code

Word or Question	Flashlight Code

Talk About It!

How is your new code different? How is it better?

Day 4

Name: _____ Date: _____

Directions: Find a dark place to test your code. Sit five or more feet (1.5 m) from your partner. Take turns using your code to ask questions. Write your questions. Write your partner's answers. Then, answer the question.

Question I Asked	My Partner's Answer

1. Was it easier to communicate with your new code?

yes   no

 Try This!

Test the flashlight code of a different partner group. See if you can follow it.

Unit 2: Light

Name: _____ Date: _____

Directions: Think about how you worked on this challenge. Draw you and your friends using your flashlight code. Then, answer the questions.

1. What was your favorite part about this challenge?

_____

— — — — — — — — — — — — — — — — — —

_____

— — — — — — — — — — — — — — — — — —

_____

2. When could you use your flashlight code?

_____

— — — — — — — — — — — — — — — — — —

_____

_____

— — — — — — — — — — — — — — — — — —

_____

Talk About It!

What science concepts did you use in this challenge?

Sound Teaching Support

Overview of Unit Activities

Students will learn about and explore how sound is created through the following activities:

- reading about and studying pictures of how sound is made and heard
- reading about and studying pictures of loud and soft sounds
- experimenting with how sound waves travel and vibrate
- making music shakers
- charting how well people hear through different materials
- creating cup phones

Materials Per Group

Week 1

- basic school supplies
- bowl
- cardboard
- clock that ticks
- metal spoon
- plastic bottle
- plastic wrap (enough to cover bowl)
- rubber bands
- sprinkles (a handful)
- stereo or speaker to play music
- various filler materials for music shaker (beans, rice, beads, paper clips, etc.)
- wooden ruler

STEAM Challenge

- basic school supplies
- fishing line (12 feet, 3.5 m)
- foam cups (2)
- paper clips (20–30)
- paper cups (2)
- plastic cups (2)
- ribbon (12 feet, 3.5 m)
- string (12 feet, 3.5 m)
- yarn (12 feet, 3.5 m)

Setup and Instructional Tips

- Set expectations for use of rubber bands (e.g., no sling shooting or placing near faces).
- **Week 1 Day 3:** Students may need help attaching the rubber band to secure the plastic wrap tightly. If speakers are not available, play music on a cell phone.
- **STEAM Challenge:** The challenge can be done individually or in groups. If students are working in groups, have students sketch their own designs first. Then, have them share designs in groups and decide on one together.
- **Week 2 Day 4:** If needed, guide students in constructing their cup phones. Poke holes in the bottom of the cups, using a pen or sharpened pencil (one in each). Pull the string through the cup, and attach a paper clip to prevent the string from pulling through.

Discussion Questions

- How do you think sound is made?
- What sounds do you hear in your home? Outside? At a store?
- What makes things sound different?
- What sounds do you like?
- How do you use sound in your everyday life?
- How can we use sound to solve problems?

Additional Notes

- **Possible Misconception:** Everything makes sound.
- **Truth:** Objects that are capable of vibrating can make sound.
- **Possible Design Solutions:** Students may try using different types of cups and string-like material between the cups. They might try to have one or multiple lengths of string-like material between cups.

Scaffolding and Extension Suggestions

- Ask students to make lists of items they find in their homes that make sound.
- Challenge students to create cup phones for three-way calling.

Answer Key

Week 1 Day 1
The following items should be circled: whistle, car, cell phone, drums

Week 1 Day 2
1. waves
2. loud
3. soft

Week 1 Day 3
1. see—sprinkles bouncing on the plastic wrap
2. hear—music playing

Week 1 Day 5
1. metal spoon
2. Probable answer will be cardboard because it is most likely to reduce the sound of the ticking clock.

Weeks 2 & 3
See STEAM Challenge Rubric on page 221.

Name: _____ Date: _____

Directions: Read the text. Study the diagram. Then, circle the things that make sound.

Many things can make sounds. Sounds are made by vibrations. Vibrations happen when things move back and forth fast. Those vibrations travel as sound waves. They travel to our ears. Then, we can hear the sound.

sound waves

Does It Make Sound?

whistle   crayons   pumpkin   car

cell phone   sandcastle   drums   hat

Name: _____ Date: _____

Directions: Read the text. Study the diagrams. Then, complete the sentences.

Sound waves can travel through air, liquid, and solid objects. Sounds can be loud and soft. Big sound waves have more energy. They make loud sounds. Small sound waves make soft sounds.

loud sound wave　　　　　**soft sound wave**

> ## Word Bank
>
> | loud | soft | waves |

_____

1. Sound _____ travel through the air.

2. When sound waves are big, the sound is _____
   _____.

3. When sound waves are small, the sound is _____
   _____.

🗨 Talk About It!

What are some examples of loud sounds?
What are some examples of soft sounds?

Name: _____ Date: _____

Directions: Follow the steps to set up a sound experiment. Use the diagram to help you. Then, answer the questions.

Steps

1. Place plastic wrap tightly over a small bowl.

2. Secure it with a rubber band.

3. Add a handful of sprinkles on top.

4. Place the bowl by a speaker.

5. Play some music.

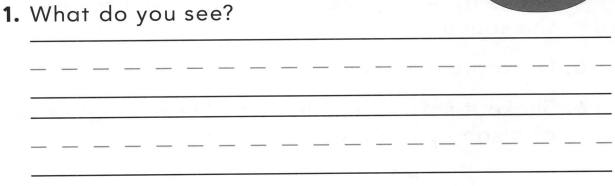

---

1. What do you see?

_____

– – – – – – – – – – – – – – – –

_____

– – – – – – – – – – – – – – – –

_____

2. What do you hear?

_____

– – – – – – – – – – – – – – – –

_____

– – – – – – – – – – – – – – – –

_____

 Talk About It!

Why do the sprinkles move?

Unit 3: Sound

Name: _____ Date: _____

Directions: Read the text. Follow the steps to make your own music shaker.

Music is made from vibrations. Instruments make different sounds.

Steps to Make a Music Shaker

1. Empty and clean a plastic bottle.

2. Add small items into the bottle. You could add beans, beads, rice, or other small things.

3. Put the top on your bottle.

4. Shake it. Add more items if you want to change the sound.

5. Decorate your shaker.

6. Shake it soft. Shake it hard. Shake it to the beat of a song you know.

Name: _____ Date: _____

Directions: Listen to how well sound travels through different solid objects. Place each item against your ear. Then, place your ear near a ticking clock. Listen for a few seconds. Mark your results. Then, answer the questions.

How Loud Is the Sound?

Object	Soft	Medium	Loud
wooden ruler			
metal spoon			
piece of cardboard			

1. Which object made the ticking sound the loudest?

_____

_ _

_____

2. You want to soundproof a room. Which material will you use? Tell why.

wood   **metal**   **cardboard**

_____

_ _

_____

_ _

_____

Name: _____ Date: _____

Directions: Read the text. Answer the questions.

The Challenge

Make a cup phone so you can talk to a friend from a distance.

Criteria

- Your cup phone must allow you to talk and listen to a person 10 feet (3 m) away.

- You must be able to hear a person whispering on the other end.

Constraint

- You may only use the materials you are given.

1. What questions do you have?

_____

_____

_____

_____

2. What are you excited about?

_____

_____

_____

_____

Name: _____ Date: _____

Directions: Read the text. Study the pictures of the cup phones. Then, answer the questions.

Cup phones have been around a long time. Some work better than others. You can learn what others have done. Then, you can add to their ideas.

Cup Phone Design 1	**Cup Phone Design 2**

1. How are these cup phones different?

_____
_ _ _ _ _ _ _ _ _ _ _ _ _ _ _ _ _ _ _ _
_____
_____
_ _ _ _ _ _ _ _ _ _ _ _ _ _ _ _ _ _ _ _
_____

2. Which design do you think works better?

Design 1   **Design 2**

Name: _____ Date: _____

Directions: Plan your cup phone. Sketch your design.

1. What type of cups will you use?

    paper   **plastic**   **foam**

2. What will you use to connect your cups?

    string   **yarn**   **fishing line**   **ribbon**
                              _____

    paper clips   other: _____

Think About It!

How will you attach the line material to the cups?

Day 4

Name: _____ Date: _____

Directions: Write who will do each job. Add jobs if you need to. Then, build your cup phone. Check off the jobs as you complete them.

✔	To Do List	Student Name(s)
	Gather materials.	
	Measure and cut materials.	
	Attach any parts.	

 Quick Tip!

If something is not working, try different materials!

Name: _____ Date:_____

Directions: Stand 10 feet (3 m) away from your partner. Whisper a sentence into your cup phone. Ask them to repeat what you said. Switch roles. Listen as they whisper a sentence to you. Then, answer the questions.

💡 **Quick Tip!**

Make sure the line between your cups is pulled tight!

1. What sentence did you whisper into your cup phone?

_____

_____

_____

_____

_____

2. What did your partner think you said?

_____

_____

_____

_____

_____

3. Based on the results, how well did your cup phone work?

not at all   okay   great

Name: _____ Date: _____

Directions: Think about your cup phone. Answer the questions. Plan how you will improve it.

1. What do you think you should keep the same about your design?

_____

- -

_____

_____

- -

_____

2. What do you think you should change about your design?

_____

- -

_____

_____

- -

_____

New Criterion Alert!

Pick at least one material to add or change. Choose from the materials given to you.

3. The material I will add or change is

_____

- -

_____.

Name: _____ Date: _____

Directions: Sketch your new cup phone design. Circle the parts or materials that are different.

Name: _____ Date: _____

Directions: Rebuild your cup phone. Make it work better. Use this chart to help you.

✔	To Do List	Student Name(s)
	Gather new materials.	
	Measure and cut materials.	
	Add new parts or pieces.	

☆ **Try This!**

Did your phone work great the first time? See if you can make it work from 20 feet (6 m) apart.

Name: _____ Date: _____

Directions: Stand 10 feet (3 m) away from your partner. Whisper a new sentence into your cup phone. Ask them to repeat what you said. Switch roles. Listen as they whisper a new sentence to you. Then, answer the questions.

1. What sentence did you whisper into your cup phone?

   _____

   _

   _____

   _

   _____

2. What did your partner think you said?

   _____

   _

   _____

   _

   _____

3. Did your new cup phone work better? Tell a friend how you know.

Try This!

Try a different group's cup phone. See if you can hear a difference.

Name: _____ Date: _____

Directions: Think about how you worked on this challenge. Draw yourself as an engineer during this challenge. Write to tell what you are doing.

_____

_ _

_____

_ _

_____

Talk About It!

What was your favorite part of this challenge?

What surprised you about this challenge?

Texture Teaching Support

Overview of Unit Activities

Students will learn about and explore different textures and their uses through the following activities:

- reading about and studying pictures of different textures
- reading about and naming different textures
- feeling objects and guessing what they are
- drawing different textures
- analyzing a graph of building materials
- creating houses with many different textures

Materials Per Group

Week 1

- art materials with different textures (e.g., beads, felt, yarn, bubble wrap, sandpaper)
- basic school supplies
- paper bag
- small objects with different textures (3–5)

STEAM Challenge

- basic school supplies
- craft sticks (20+)
- dry cereal (ring-shaped; a handful or more)
- foil
- modeling clay
- paper clips (10+)
- piece of cardboard (10" × 10", 25 cm x 25 cm)
- pipe cleaners (10+)
- sandpaper (1–2 sheets)
- sugar cubes (20+)
- tissue paper (1–2 sheets)

Setup and Instructional Tips

- **Materials:** It is especially true for this challenge that materials options are flexible. The goal is to provide options that have a variety of different textures.
- **Week 1 Day 3:** To save class time, you may choose to prepare mystery bags for students ahead of time. Place 3–5 objects with different textures in each bag.
- **STEAM Challenge:** The challenge can be done individually or in groups. If students are working in groups, have students sketch their own designs first. Then, have them share designs in groups and decide on one together.

Discussion Questions

- What is texture?
- What are some ways we can use different textures?
- Name some textures near you.
- What textures do you like to feel?
- How are textures important to artists and engineers?

Additional Notes

- **Possible Misconception:** If an object is not rough or bumpy, it does not have a texture.
- **Truth:** All objects can be classified by texture. Soft or smooth objects will not feel rough or bumpy.
- **Possible Design Solutions:** Students may build houses using craft sticks as the main support. They might add materials with different textures as they see fit.

Scaffolding and Extension Suggestions

- Support students in designing houses by showing them images of simple house structures that they can copy.
- Challenge students to create two-story structures.

Answer Key

Week 1 Day 1
The following items should be circled: desk, window, tablet, spoon

1. B

Week 1 Day 2
Examples:
dog—hairy
tennis ball—fuzzy
brick—rough
bone—smooth

Week 1 Day 5
1. brick
2. glass
3. rough/hard
4. smooth

Weeks 2 & 3
See STEAM Challenge Rubric on page 221.

Day 1

Name: _____ Date: _____

Directions: Read the text. Circle the objects that have smooth textures. Then, answer the question.

All objects have one or more textures. Texture is something you can see and feel. Smooth and bumpy are types of textures. Textures are used in different ways. A blanket might have a soft texture. A road might have a rough texture.

1. Texture is something you _____ .

(A) see and hear

(B) see and feel

(C) feel and smell

(D) smell and hear

Name: _____ Date: _____

Directions: Read the text. Study the picture. Label the textures in the picture. Then, answer the question.

Day 2

We can describe things by telling how they feel. We can use words that describe textures. There are many textures all around us. Which ones do you see? Which ones can you feel?

Texture Words

| fuzzy | hairy | rough | smooth |

_____   _____

- - - - - - - - - - - - - - - -   - - - - - - - - - - - - - - - -

_____   _____

_____   _____

- - - - - - - - - - - - - - - -   - - - - - - - - - - - - - - - -

_____   _____

1. Add an object to the picture above. What texture does it have?

_____

- -

_____

Name: _____ Date: _____

Directions: Place a few objects in a bag. Trade with a friend. Put your hand in the bag. Feel the objects, but do not look at them. Try to guess what each one is. Write your guesses in the chart. Then, look in the bag, and complete the chart. Answer the question.

Texture of Object	Your Guess	Name of Object
1.		
2.		
3.		
4.		
5.		

6. What was your favorite texture in the bag?

_____

- -

_____

Day 4

Name: _____ Date: _____

Directions: Make a picture that has many textures. Use different fabrics and other materials. Glue them on the page. If you want, make a funny self-portrait. It does not have to look real. Be creative or even silly!

 Try This!

Find a partner. Trade pictures. Close your eyes, and feel the picture they made. Feel all the textures. Try and guess what their picture is.

Day 5

Name: _____ Date: _____

Directions: Study the bar graph. Then, answer the questions.

Pieces of Materials Needed to Build a House

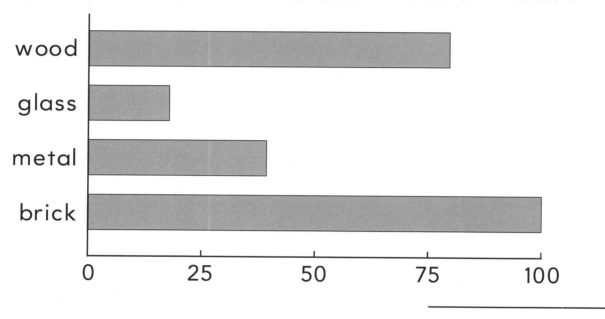

1. Which material was used the most? _____

2. Which material was used the least? _____

3. Describe the texture of wood and brick.

   _____

   _____

   _____

4. Describe the texture of glass and metal.

   _____

   _____

   _____

29644—180 Days: Hands-On STEAM

Name: _____ Date: _____

Directions: Read the text. Then, answer the question.

The Challenge

Imagine you build homes. A new client loves textures. They want a lot of them. Build a house with as many textures as you can.

Criteria

- The house must have three or more textures.
- The house must stand on its own.
- The house must have a window, a door, and a roof.

Constraints

- You may only use the materials you are given.
- The home must fit on the piece of cardboard given to you.

1. How do you feel about this challenge? Color one or more.

excited   worried   interested   unsure

 Quick Tip!

You can make your own textures! Glue items onto paper or cardboard. Try it with cereal or string.

Day 2

Name: _____ Date: _____

Directions: Think about the parts of a house. Write ideas in the circles. Then, complete the task.

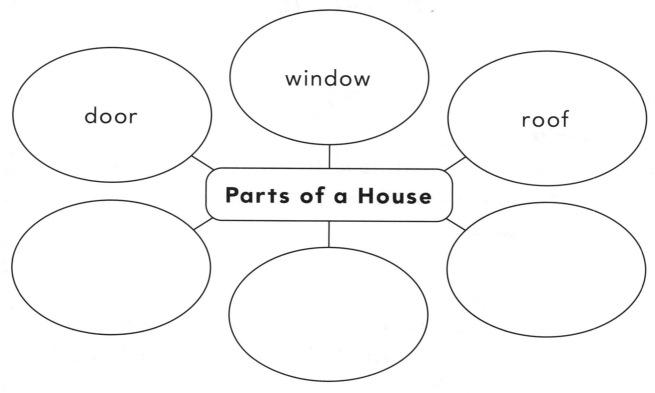

door

window

roof

Parts of a House

Task: Look at the materials that you have been given. List all the textures you see.

Name: _____ Date: _____

Directions: Plan your design. Sketch your house.
Label the materials used for each part.

1. What textures will be in your house? You must
have three or more.

_____   _____

- - - - - - - - -   - - - - - - - - -

_____   _____

_____   _____

- - - - - - - - -   - - - - - - - - -

_____   _____

2. Will you make any of your own textures?

yes   **no**

3. How will you hold the pieces together?

_____

- -

_____

_____

- -

_____

Name: _____ Date: _____

Directions: Write who will do each job. Add jobs if you need to. Then, build your house. Check off the jobs as you complete them.

✔	To Do List	Student Name(s)
	Gather materials.	
	Construct walls.	
	Make door and windows.	
	Construct roof.	
	Measure and cut parts.	
	Tape and glue parts.	

 Quick Tip!

If something is not working, try a different material!

Name: _____ Date: _____

Directions: Place your house on a flat surface. See if it stands on its own. Mark the criteria that you met. Then, answer the question.

House Criteria

☐ The house has three or more textures.

☐ The house stands on its own.

☐ The house has a window.

☐ The house has a door.

☐ The house has a roof.

1. What textures can be found in your house? List them.

_____   _____

- - - - - - - - - - - - - -   - - - - - - - - - - - - - -

_____   _____

- - - - - - - - - - - - - -   - - - - - - - - - - - - - -

_____   _____

- - - - - - - - - - - - - -   - - - - - - - - - - - - - -

_____   _____

Day 1

Name: _____ Date: _____

Directions: Think about your house design. Answer the questions. Then, plan how you will improve it.

1. Did your house turn out how you planned?

yes   **no**

2. Draw two house designs that you saw from other groups. Put a checkmark by your favorite.

☐ **Design 1**	☐ **Design 2**

New Criterion Alert!

Add at least one more new texture.

3. What texture would you like to add? Where do you want to add it?

_____

_____

_____

_____

Name: _____ Date: _____

Directions: Sketch your new design. Label all the textures. Circle any new ones.

Unit 4: Texture

Name: _____ Date: _____

Directions: Rebuild your house. Make it better. Use this chart to help you.

✓	To Do List	Student Name(s)
	Gather new materials.	
	Add new textures.	
	Remove parts and materials that did not work.	
	Change or add parts of the house.	
	Measure and cut materials.	
	Tape and glue parts and pieces.	

Name: _____ Date: _____

Directions: Place your house on a flat surface. See if it stands on its own. Mark the criteria that you met. Then, answer the question.

House Criteria

☐ The house has four or more textures.

☐ The house stands on its own.

☐ The house has a window.

☐ The house has a door.

☐ The house has a roof.

1. What textures can be found in your house? List them.

_____   _____

_ _ _ _ _ _ _ _ _ _ _   _ _ _ _ _ _ _ _ _ _ _

_____   _____

_ _ _ _ _ _ _ _ _ _ _   _ _ _ _ _ _ _ _ _ _ _

_____   _____

_ _ _ _ _ _ _ _ _ _ _   _ _ _ _ _ _ _ _ _ _ _

_____   _____

Day 5

Name: _____ Date: _____

Directions: Think about how you worked on this challenge. Draw yourself as an engineer. Show how you worked on different parts of this challenge.

This is me planning.	This is me building.
This is me testing.	This is me working with others.

Talk About It!

What textures would you want in your home?

Animal Inspiration Teaching Support

Overview of Unit Activities

Students will learn about and explore how animal structures inspire new ideas through the following activities:

- reading about and studying pictures of animal body parts
- reading about and studying inventions inspired by animal body parts
- trying to camouflage objects outside
- drawing inventions inspired by animals
- charting ways animal body parts are helpful
- creating inventions inspired by bird body parts

Materials Per Group

Week 1

- basic school supplies
- paper bags
- small objects that can be placed in a paper bag to camouflage (5)

STEAM Challenge

- basic school supplies
- cardboard tubes (3–4)
- clothespins (5–10)
- construction paper (2–3 sheets)
- cotton balls (15–20)
- craft sticks (10–20)
- felt (1–2 sheets)
- foil
- googly eyes
- hot glue gun (optional)
- note cards (5–10)
- pictures of different birds (3+)
- pipe cleaners (5–10)
- plastic wrap
- straws (3–4)

Setup and Instructional Tips

- **Week 1 Day 3:** This is an outdoor activity, so plan accordingly with the weather. To save class time, you may prepare the paper bags with items to camouflage ahead of time.
- **STEAM Challenge:** The challenge can be done individually or in groups. If students are working in groups, have students sketch their own designs first. Then, have them share designs in groups and decide on one together.
- **Materials:** A hot glue gun may come in handy. You may offer this as an option and have students tell you what they want glued.

Discussion Questions

- What are external structures?
- How do animals survive in the wild?
- What structures do people have that help them survive?
- How have animals inspired new ideas?
- What can we learn from animals?

Additional Notes

- **Possible Misconception:** Not all body parts serve a purpose.
  Truth: Each body part—internal and external, human and animal—serves a purpose.
- **Possible Design Solutions:** Students will make inventions that mimic body parts of birds (e.g., feathers—warm covering of a blanket or coat, beak—a tool for reaching or grabbing, webbed feet—flippers for swimming).

Scaffolding and Extension Suggestions

- Support students with invention ideas by having them search in books or online for inventions inspired by birds.
- Challenge students to create inventions based on specific birds with very unique structures.

Answer Key

Week 1 Day 1
1. C
2. A

Week 1 Day 2
fish tail—swimming fins
sheep wool—jacket
turtle shell—helmet
bird wings—drone

Week 1 Day 3
3. Example: Camouflage helps animals hide from predators.

Week 1 Day 5
alligator—teeth; food (or skin; protection)
armadillo—shell-like skin; protection
monkey—tail; movement
bear—claws; food or protection

1. Best answers: armadillo, alligator, or bear. Other answers may be accepted if students can explain why.

Weeks 2 & 3
See STEAM Challenge Rubric on page 221.

Name: _____ Date: _____

Directions: Read the text. Study the pictures. Then, answer the questions.

All animals have parts. They have parts on the inside. They have parts on the outside. An animal's body parts help it live. They help it survive. Each animal part serves a purpose.

Fish have tails. They use them to swim.

Birds have wings. They use them to fly.

Giraffes have long necks. This helps them reach food in high trees.

1. Animals have parts _____ .

   (A) inside their bodies only

   (B) outside their bodies only

   (C) inside and outside their bodies

2. Why do fish have tails?

   (A) to swim

   (B) to fly

   (C) to eat

Name: _____ Date: _____

Directions: Read the text. Draws lines to match the animal parts to the inventions.

People can get ideas from animals. They look at their parts. They learn how they work. Then, they make new things. Think about turtles. They have hard shells. Their shells protect them. People do not have shells. So, they made some! People wear helmets to protect their heads. What other ideas come from animals?

Animal Parts

Inventions

Talk About It!

What other things do you think were inspired by animal parts?

Name: _____ Date: _____

Directions: Read the text. Complete the task. Then, answer the questions.

> Some animals can blend in with things around them. They use camouflage. People have made ways to camouflage. Put five objects in a bag. Go outside. Try to put the objects in places where they blend in.
>
>

1. Which objects were easy to blend in?

_____

_____

2. Which objects were hard to blend in?

_____

_____

3. How might camouflage help an animal?

_____

_____

_____

Day 4

Name: _____ Date: _____

Directions: Draw an animal of your choice. Then, draw an invention inspired by your animal. It can be realistic. Or, it can be imaginary.

Animal

Invention

Name: _____ Date: _____

Directions: Study the animals in the chart. Write one useful body part you see. Write an *X* to show how it helps the animal. Then, answer the question.

Animal	Useful Body Part	How It Helps		
		Protection	Movement	Food
	wings		X	

1. You want to make something to protect yourself. Which animals would you look at for ideas?

bird   alligator   armadillo   monkey   bear

Day 1

Name: _____ Date: _____

Directions: Read the text. Then, answer the question.

The Challenge

You are an inventor. Look to birds for inspiration. Invent something that solves a problem or meets a need. It might be a toy, a tool, or something else.

Criteria

- The invention must be inspired by one or more bird body parts (beak, wings, etc.).

- The invention must solve a problem or meet a need.

Constraint

- You may only use the materials you are given.

1. What questions do you have?

_____

_ _

_____

_ _

_____

🗨 Talk About It!

What are some birds you know of? What do they look like? What is special about them?

Name: _____ Date: _____

Directions: Think about the structures, or body parts, birds have. Write or draw ideas in the circles. Then, answer the questions.

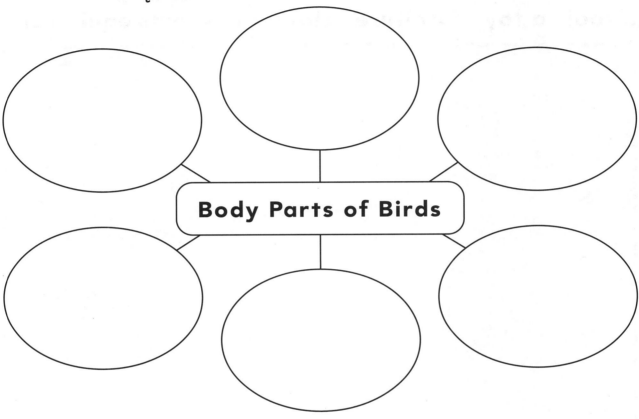

Body Parts of Birds

1. What bird body part will you use for inspiration?

_____

- - - - - - - - - - - - - - - - - - -

_____

2. What ideas do you have for an invention?

_____

- - - - - - - - - - - - - - - - - - -

_____

- - - - - - - - - - - - - - - - - - -

_____

Name: _____ Date: _____

Directions: Answer the question. Sketch your design.

1. What type of invention will you make?

a tool   a toy   furniture   clothing   sports equipment

Name: _____ Date: _____

Directions: Write who will do each job. Add jobs if you need to. Then, build your invention. Check off the jobs as you complete them.

✓	To Do List	Student Name(s)
	Gather materials.	
	Measure and cut materials.	
	Tape and glue parts.	

 Talk About It!

How well did your team work together?

Name: _____ Date: _____

Directions: Share your invention with others. Plan what you will tell them. Then, show them how it works. Write what they say.

Tell

1. What does your invention do?

_____

- -

_____

2. What bird structure did you use for inspiration?

_____

- -

_____

3. Who might want to use your invention?

_____

- -

_____

Show

4. Model how your invention works. Point out the parts that were inspired by birds.

Ask

5. How can I make it better?

_____

- -

_____

_____

- -

_____

Day 1

Name: _____ Date: _____

Directions: Think about the product you made. Answer the questions. Plan on how you will improve it.

1. Did your invention turn out how you planned?

   yes   **no**

2. Do you need to change the shape?

   yes   **no**

3. Do you need to change the size?

   yes   **no**

4. Do you need new materials?

   yes   **no**

5. What else could you add or change to make it better? Write or draw some ideas.

Unit 5: Animal Inspiration

Name: _____ Date: _____

Directions: Sketch your new design. Circle the parts that are different or new. Then, answer the question.

1. Do you think this design will work better? How confident are you?

**not very
confident**   **a little
confident**   **very
confident**

Name: _____ Date: _____

Directions: Rebuild your invention. Make it better.
Use this chart to help you.

✔	To Do List	Student Name(s)
	Gather new materials.	
	Change or remove unwanted parts.	
	Add new parts or features.	
	Measure and cut materials.	
	Tape and glue parts.	

Name: _____ Date: _____

Directions: Share your invention with others. Plan what you will tell them. Then, show them how it works. Write what they say.

Tell

1. What changes did you make?

_____
- -
_____
- -
_____

2. Why do you think it is better?

_____
- -
_____
- -
_____

Show

3. Model how your invention works. Point out the parts that were inspired by birds. Point out the changes you made.

Ask

4. What do you like about the new design?

_____
- -
_____

Name: _____ Date: _____

Directions: Think about how you worked on this challenge. Draw yourself as an engineer. Show how you worked on different parts of this challenge.

This is me planning.	This is me building.
This is me testing.	This is me working with others.

☆ **Try This!**

Think of the inventions made in class. Which was your favorite? Try to make your own version of it. Try to make it better.

Plant Inspiration Teaching Support

Overview of Unit Activities

Students will learn about and explore structures and functions of plants through the following activities:

- reading about and studying how plant structures have inspired inventions
- dissecting a flower and sketching its parts
- designing plants
- identifying parts of plants they could mimic
- creating floating towns inspired by plant structures

Materials Per Group

Week 1

- basic school supplies
- flower to dissect (1)

STEAM Challenge

- basic school supplies
- balloons (2–4)
- craft sticks
- toothpicks (4–6)
- resealable plastic bags (2)
- small toy people (3–5)
- straws (2–4)
- timer
- tub of water

Setup and Instructional Tips

- **Week 1 Day 3:** Prepare a model of a dissected flower to show as an example.
- **STEAM Challenge:** The challenge can be done individually or in groups. If students are working in groups, have students sketch their own designs first. Then, have them share designs in groups and decide on one together.
- **Testing Days:** Prepare a tub of water for students to test their floating towns.

Discussion Questions

- What are some external structures of plants?
- How do plants survive in different environments?
- What plant parts help protect plants?

- What are some of your favorite plants?
- What can we learn from different plants and their structures?
- What inventions were inspired by plant structures?

Additional Notes

- **Possible Misconceptions:** Plant parts that look pretty (such as petals) do not serve a purpose.
- **Truth:** All plant parts serve a purpose. Even looking pretty is serving a purpose if it attracts pollinators.
- **Possible Design Solutions:** Students might try to create pockets of air with balloons or plastic bags to help their towns float. They might make the parts of their towns shaped like the leaves of water lilies. They might connect the town with craft sticks or straws.

Scaffolding and Extension Suggestions

- Allow students to first create floating cities with only one part.
- Challenge students to use at least two different methods to make their towns float.

Answer Key

Week 1 Day 1
dandelion—parachute
briar patch plant—barbed wire
tree—umbrella
leaf—solar panels

Week 1 Day 2
1. Examples: cactus, rose
2. Examples: shoes, pants, bags/backpacks, straps

Week 1 Day 5
1. Answers may include cactus spines or rose thorns.

Weeks 2 & 3
See STEAM Challenge Rubric on page 221.

Name: _____ Date: _____

Directions: Read the text. Draw lines to match the plants to the inventions.

Plants are made of different parts. These parts help them live. They help them survive in different places. Plants have roots, stems, and leaves. Some plants have flowers. Some flowers grow fruit. Plants can inspire new ideas. They can help us solve problems.

Plants

Inventions

Name: _____ Date: _____

Directions: Read the text. Study the pictures. Then, answer the questions.

Some plants have parts that are unique. Look at the cocklebur plant. It has parts called *burs*. They are prickly and shaped like hooks. The burs have seeds in them. The burs attach to animals and people. This helps seeds travel to different places.

Velcro® is a special material. We use it to connect two things. It was inspired, or based on, the burs of cocklebur plants.

1. What other plants have spiky or prickly parts?

_____

_ _

_____

2. What are three things we use Velcro® for?

_____   _____

_ _ _ _ _ _ _ _ _   _ _ _ _ _ _ _ _ _

_____   _____

_____

_ _ _ _ _ _ _ _ _

_____

Name: _____ Date: _____

Directions: Take apart a flower. Look at all the parts.
Sketch each part. Then, answer the questions.

1. What are the colors and textures of the flower?

_____

_ _ _ _ _ _ _ _ _ _ _ _ _ _ _ _ _ _ _

_____

_____

_ _ _ _ _ _ _ _ _ _ _ _ _ _ _ _ _ _ _

_____

2. What is the shape of the flower? How might the shape be helpful?

_____

_ _ _ _ _ _ _ _ _ _ _ _ _ _ _ _ _ _ _

_____

_____

_ _ _ _ _ _ _ _ _ _ _ _ _ _ _ _ _ _ _

_____

Talk About It!

How could you mimic, or copy, parts of the flower
to make something new?

Day 4

Name: _____ Date: _____

Directions: Design your own plant. Complete the sentences. Draw it, and label the parts of your plant. Be creative!

_____

My plant lives _____.

The name of my plant is _____.

My plant is special because _____

_____.

Unit 6: Plant Inspiration

Name: _____ Date: _____

Directions: Study the pictures. Look closely at the plant parts. Write which part you would want to mimic. Then, answer the question.

Plant	Picture	Useful Part to Mimic (copy)
rose		
cactus		
tree		
water lily		

1. You want to make some type of protection. Which plant and part could you mimic?

_____

_ _

_____

Name: _____ Date: _____

Directions: Read the text. Then, study the example.

The Challenge

Design a town that can float on water. Make a model of your floating town.

Criteria

- Your design must use ideas from parts of a floating plant.

- Your design must float in a tub of water.

- Your design must have three parts that connect. Each part must float on its own.

Constraint

- You may only use the materials you are given.

Example

This is a design for a floating city. Can you see the different parts? They float on their own. They connect to each other with bridges.

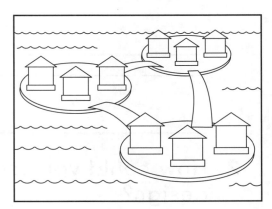

Talk About It!

What questions do you have about this challenge?

Day 2

Name: _____ Date: _____

Directions: Plants that float have special parts. Read the text about floating plants. Study the pictures. Then, answer the questions.

Fresh Water Plant	Saltwater Plant
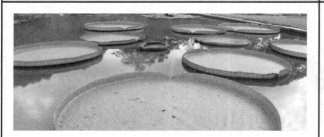	
Water lilies have air in their leaf veins. It helps them float. The leaf shape and size also help it float.	Kelp has small, round parts that have air inside. They help it float.

1. How could you use air in your design?

_____

_____

_____

_____

2. How could you use the plant shapes in your design?

_____

_____

_____

_____

Name: _____ Date: _____

Directions: Sketch your floating town design. Write the materials you plan to use.

Materials

_____   _____   _____

_____   _____   _____

_____   _____   _____

Name: _____ Date: _____

Directions: Write who will do each job. Add jobs if you need to. Then, build your floating town. Check off the jobs as you complete them.

✔	To Do List	Student Name(s)
	Gather materials.	
	Make part one.	
	Make part two.	
	Make part three.	
	Measure and cut materials.	
	Tape and glue parts.	

💡 **Quick Tip!**

It is okay to do a few mini tests as you build! Get a bowl of water. Check that each part floats.

Name: _____ Date: _____

Directions: Place your floating town in a tub of water. Wait at least 1 minute. Then, answer the questions.

Does your floating town...	yes/no
float?	
have a plant-like structure?	
have three parts?	
include ideas from all team members?	

 Try This!

The ocean is not always calm. Move the tub back and forth a little. Does your town still float?

Unit 6: Plant Inspiration

Name: _____ Date: _____

Directions: Think about your floating town. Answer the questions. Then, plan how you will improve it.

1. What part of your design worked well?

_____

- - - - - - - - - - - - - - - - - - - -

_____

2. What do you need to change or add to make it better?

_____

- - - - - - - - - - - - - - - - - - - -

_____

_____

- - - - - - - - - - - - - - - - - - - -

_____

New Criterion Alert!

Each part of your town must support a small toy person. They must stay afloat. You will add them when you retest your design.

3. What do you need to add or change to meet this new criterion?

_____

- - - - - - - - - - - - - - - - - - - -

_____

_____

- - - - - - - - - - - - - - - - - - - -

_____

Name: _____ Date: _____

Directions: Sketch your new design. Circle the parts that are new or different. List any new materials you will use.

Materials

_____   _____   _____

- - - - - - - - - - - -   - - - - - - - - - - - -   - - - - - - - - - - - -

_____   _____   _____

_____   _____   _____

- - - - - - - - - - - -   - - - - - - - - - - - -   - - - - - - - - - - - -

Name: _____ Date: _____

Directions: Rebuild your floating town. Make it better. Use this chart to help you.

✔	To Do List	Student Name(s)
	Gather new materials.	
	Change or remove unwanted parts.	
	Add new features.	
	Measure and cut materials.	
	Tape and glue parts.	

Name: _____ Date: _____

Directions: Place your floating town in a tub of water. Place a small toy person on each part of your town. Wait at least 1 minute. Then, answer the questions.

Does your floating town...	yes/no
stay afloat with the people on it?	
have a plant-like structure?	
have three parts?	
include ideas from all team members?	

 Try This!

The ocean is not always calm. Move the tub back and forth a little. Do the toy people stay on?

Name: _____ Date: _____

Directions: Think about how you worked on this challenge. Give your town a name. Draw yourself in your town.

_____

- -

Town Name: _____

```
┌ ─ ─ ─ ─ ─ ─ ─ ─ ─ ─ ─ ─ ─ ─ ─ ─ ┐

│                                  │

│                                  │

│                                  │

│                                  │

│                                  │

│                                  │

│                                  │

└ ─ ─ ─ ─ ─ ─ ─ ─ ─ ─ ─ ─ ─ ─ ─ ─ ┘
```

💡 **Talk About It!**

What would be fun about living in a floating town?

What would be hard about living in a floating town?

Signs and Signals Teaching Support

Overview of Unit Activities

Students will learn about and explore signs and signals animals make to communicate through the following activities:

- reading about and studying how baby animals communicate
- reading about and studying how animals help their young
- sorting pictures of animal parents caring for their young
- acting out how animal parents care for their young
- studying a map of animals around the world
- creating bridges to help an adult animal rescue its baby

Materials Per Group

Week 1
- basic school supplies

STEAM Challenge
- basic school supplies
- cardboard tubes (4–6)
- cardstock (2–4 pieces)
- craft sticks (10–20+)
- limes (2)
- orange (1)
- paper plates (2)
- pipe cleaners (10–15)
- string (2–4 feet, 1 m)

Setup and Instructional Tips

- **STEAM Challenge:** The challenge can be done individually or in groups. If students are working in groups, have students sketch their own designs first. Then, have them share designs in groups and decide on one together.

- **Week 2 Day 1:** Have students color their paper plates blue or cover them with blue paper to represent ponds.

Unit 7: Signs and Signals

Discussion Questions

- How does your family take care of you?
- Why do some baby animals need help getting food?
- What kinds of things might animals teach their offspring?
- Have you ever seen animals taking care of their babies? What were they doing?
- How are animal babies and human babies the same? How are they different?
- How do animal babies let their parents know they need something? How do human babies?

Additional Notes

- **Possible Misconception:** Animal babies stay with their parents for long periods of time. **Truth:** The length of time varies depending on the animal. Some stay for short periods of time, and others stay much longer. Some animals do not stay to care for their young.
- **Possible Design Solutions:** Students might use cardboard tubes on the ends. They might use craft sticks or pipe cleaners to connect the ends of their bridges.

Scaffolding and Extension Suggestions

- Support students by choosing smaller and lighter fruits to represent the animals.
- Challenge students to remove one type of building material, or switch it for a different material.

Answer Key

Week 1 Day 1
bird—chirp
human baby—cry
kitten—meow
elephant—trumpet

Week 1 Day 2
1. carry
2. Crocodiles carry their young in their mouths to keep them safe.

Week 1 Day 3
feeding—bird, human, dog
carrying—kangaroo, lion, gorilla
protecting—cheetah, elephant

Week 1 Day 5
1. Africa
2. Examples: tiger, panda

Weeks 2 & 3
See STEAM Challenge Rubric on page 221.

Name: _____ Date: _____

Directions: Read the text. Draw lines to match the animal babies with the sounds they make.

Day 1

Many baby animals need help from their parents. Animal parents feed their young. They protect them. They teach them. Baby animals make sounds when they need or want things. Animal parents hear the sounds. They know they must help their young.

Baby Animal	**Animal Sound**
	trumpet
	meow
	chirp
	cry

🗨 Talk About It!

What might these baby animals need when they make these sounds?

What do you say or do when you need something from an adult?

Day 2

Name: _____ Date: _____

Directions: Read the text. Study the picture. Then, answer the questions.

Animals help their young get food. They help them stay safe and warm. Some animals carry their young from place to place. This gives them time to learn and grow. Crocodiles carry their young on their backs or in their mouths. They are very careful not to hurt them. This keeps the babies safe from other animals that might eat them.

_____

1. Some animals _____ their young from place to place.

2. Why do crocodiles carry their young in their mouths?

_____

_____

_____

3. How do humans help their babies live and learn?

_____

_____

Name: _____ Date: _____

Directions: Study the pictures. Cut and paste each picture into the correct column.

How Is the Parent Helping?

Feeding	
Carrying	
Protecting	

Day 4

Name: _____ Date: _____

Directions: Work with a partner. Choose a type of animal. One of you will be the parent. The other will be the baby. Draw how the animal parent cares for its young. Then, act it out in front of others. See if they can guess what type of animal you are.

Animal: _____

This is how the animal parent cares for its young.

Name: _____ Date: _____

Directions: Study the map. Then, answer the questions.

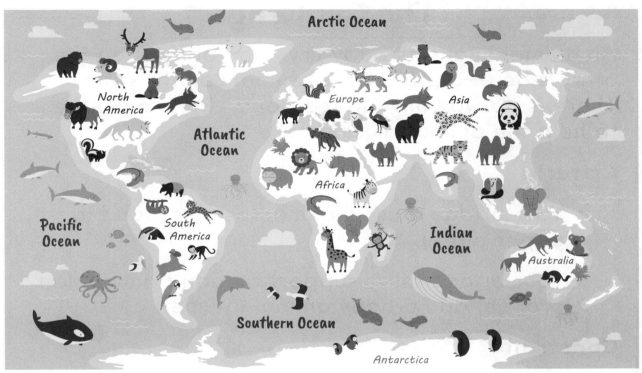

1. Where could we travel to see zebras and their young in the wild?

_____

_ _ _ _ _ _ _ _ _ _ _ _ _ _ _ _ _ _ _ _

_____

2. What are two animals you could see in Asia?

_____

_ _ _ _ _ _ _ _ _ _ _ _ _ _ _ _ _ _ _ _

_____

Talk About It!

Where would you like to travel?
What animals would you see there?

Name: _____ Date: _____

Directions: Read the text. Then, answer the question.

The Challenge

An animal hears its baby cry. The baby is on the other side of a pond. The animal cannot swim. There is no way around the pond. Build a bridge to help the animal cross safely.

Criteria

- Your bridge must reach across the pond (a paper plate).

- Your bridge must support an adult animal (an orange) and a baby animal (a lime).

Constraint

- You may only use the materials you are given.

1. Write the challenge in your own words.

_____

_ _ _ _ _ _ _ _ _ _ _ _ _ _ _ _ _ _

_____

_ _ _ _ _ _ _ _ _ _ _ _ _ _ _ _ _ _

_____

Talk About It!

Have you seen or been on any bridges? What did they look like?

Name: _____ Date: _____

Directions: Read the text. Study the pictures. Then, answer the questions.

Some bridges are human-made. Some are natural. The Golden Gate Bridge is a human-made bridge. The other bridge is a natural bridge in Utah.

1. What do the bridges have in common?

_____

- -

_____

_____

- -

_____

2. How are they different?

_____

- -

_____

_____

- -

_____

Name: _____ Date: _____

Directions: Read the questions. Think carefully.
Sketch your bridge.

 Think About It!

How long does the bridge need to be?
How tall will the bridge be?
How wide does the bridge need to be?
What materials will work best?

Name: _____ Date: _____

Directions: Write who will do each job. Add jobs if you need to. Then, build your bridge. Check off the jobs as you complete them.

✔	To Do List	Student Name(s)
	Gather materials.	
	Build your bridge.	
	Measure and cut materials.	
	Tape and glue parts.	

💡 **Quick Tip!**

It is okay to do a few mini tests as you build! Place the orange on your bridge a few times to check if it is strong enough.

Name: _____ Date: _____

Directions: Place your bridge over the pond (a paper plate). Place the adult animal (an orange) on the bridge. Place the baby animal (a lime) on the bridge. Then, answer the questions.

Does your bridge...	yes/no
reach all the way across the pond?	
stay above the pond?	
support the adult animal?	
support the baby animal?	

Talk About It!

Would your bridge stay up in bad weather? Why or why not?

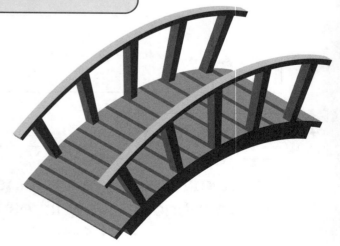

Name: _____ Date: _____

Directions: Think about your bridge. Answer the questions. Then, plan how you will improve it.

1. Did your bridge turn out how you planned?

   yes   **no**

2. What part of your bridge do you like best?

   _____

   ‒ ‒ ‒ ‒ ‒ ‒ ‒ ‒ ‒ ‒ ‒ ‒ ‒ ‒ ‒ ‒ ‒ ‒ ‒

   _____

   _____

   ‒ ‒ ‒ ‒ ‒ ‒ ‒ ‒ ‒ ‒ ‒ ‒ ‒ ‒ ‒ ‒ ‒ ‒ ‒

   _____

3. What do you need to add or change to make it work better?

   _____

   ‒ ‒ ‒ ‒ ‒ ‒ ‒ ‒ ‒ ‒ ‒ ‒ ‒ ‒ ‒ ‒ ‒ ‒ ‒

   _____

   _____

   ‒ ‒ ‒ ‒ ‒ ‒ ‒ ‒ ‒ ‒ ‒ ‒ ‒ ‒ ‒ ‒ ‒ ‒ ‒

   _____

New Criterion Alert!

You can choose how you will improve your design. Draw a star next to one.

- It will be able to support one more baby animal (lime).

- It will reach over a wider pond (2 paper plates).

Day 2

Name: _____ Date: _____

Directions: Sketch your new design. Complete the sentence.

I think this design will work better because

_____

_____

_____

_____

Name: _____ Date: _____

Directions: Rebuild your bridge. Make it better. Use this chart to help you.

✔	To Do List	Student Name(s)
	Gather materials.	
	Remove or change parts.	
	Add parts to make it stronger.	
	Measure and cut materials.	
	Tape and glue parts.	

Week 3

Day 4

Name: _____ Date: _____

Directions: Place your bridge over the pond (one or two paper plates). Place the adult animal (an orange) on the bridge. Place the baby animal (a lime) on the bridge. Then, answer the questions.

Does your bridge...	yes/no
reach all the way across the pond?	
stay above the pond?	
support the adult animal?	
support the baby animal?	
support a second baby animal? (optional)	

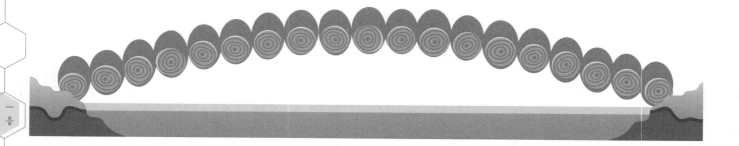

Name: _____ Date: _____

Directions: Think about how you worked on this challenge. Draw yourself as an engineer. Show how you tested your bridge.

 Talk About It!

What are other ways engineers can help animals?

Traits Teaching Support

Overview of Unit Activities

Students will learn about and explore how animals share some traits with their offspring through the following activities:

- matching plants and animals with their offspring
- reading about and studying how plants and animals pass traits onto their offspring
- sorting plants and animals
- drawing new animals with different traits
- comparing and contrasting a baby and adult animal
- creating toy animal families that share traits

Materials Per Group

Week 1

- basic school supplies
- *Plant and Animal Card Set* (Digital Resources)

STEAM Challenge

- basic school supplies
- beads (10–20)
- buttons (10–20)
- construction paper (3–4 sheets; various colors)
- craft sticks (10–20)
- googly eyes (6–12)
- modeling clay
- pipe cleaners (10–20)
- toothpicks (10–20)

Setup and Instructional Tips

- **Week 1 Day 3:** Distribute *Plant and Animal Card Set* before students begin this activity. Have them cut apart the cards and sort them. To save time, you may choose to distribute the cards pre-cut.
- **STEAM Challenge:** The challenge can be done individually or in groups. If students are working in groups, have students sketch their own designs first. Then, have them share designs in groups and decide on one together.

Discussion Questions

- How would you define *trait*?
- What are plant and animal offspring?
- How are plants and animals alike?
- How are plants and animals different?
- Do all offspring look like their parents?
- Why is it important to understand plant and animal traits?

Additional Notes

- **Possible Misconception:** Not all plants and animals have offspring.
  Truth: All species of plants and animals reproduce in some way or another. Not every individual has offspring.

- **Possible Design Solutions:** Students will invent new types of animals. The offspring they make will show some traits from its parents. They should not look exactly the same.

Scaffolding and Extension Suggestions

- Show students pictures of animal litters. Have students compare the similarities and differences between the siblings.

- Challenge students to add a moving part to each of their toys.

Answer Key

Week 1 Day 1
dog—puppy
apple tree—seedling
cat—kitten
rose—rose bud

Week 1 Day 2
1. Answers may include that the fawn is too young to have antlers, or the fawn might be female.
2. Examples: brown hair, curly hair, freckles, long legs, green eyes

Week 1 Day 5
1. Example: The chick will grow bigger. It will grow more feathers. It will change colors.

Weeks 2 & 3
See STEAM Challenge Rubric on page 221.

Day 1

Name: _____ Date: _____

Directions: Read the text. Draw lines to match the parent to its offspring.

All plants and animals reproduce. They make more of the same type of plant or animal. These new plants or animals are called *offspring*. In animals, these are the babies. Offspring often look and act like their parents. They share traits. Traits are passed down from the parent to the offspring.

Parent   **Offspring**

⭐ **Try This!**

Can you think of other parents and their offspring? It could be plants or animals. Draw them on a sheet of paper. Circle the parts that are similar.

Name: _____ Date: _____

Directions: Read the text. Study the pictures. Then, answer the questions.

> All plants and animals have unique traits. Traits are how living things look or act. Hair color is a trait. Height is a trait. Most traits are passed down from parents to offspring. This is why offspring look like their parents. Animals get traits from both parents. Some traits can change as living things grow.

parent—adult male deer   offspring—fawn

1. Why do you think the young deer doesn't have antlers like its parent?

_____

_ _ _ _ _ _ _ _ _ _ _ _ _ _ _

_____

_ _ _ _ _ _ _ _ _ _ _ _ _ _ _

_____

2. What are some of your traits?

_____

_ _ _ _ _ _ _ _ _ _ _ _ _ _ _

_____

_ _ _ _ _ _ _ _ _ _ _ _ _ _ _

_____

Name: _____ Date: _____

Directions: Cut out the plant and animal cards. Sort the cards into groups. Sort them in a few different ways. Write the categories you made. Write the plants and animals you put in each group.

Categories (Examples: fur, no fur)	Plants and Animals in Group

Talk About It!

Compare your categories with others. Which ones were most common?

Name: _____ Date: _____

Directions: Think of different traits you have learned about. Invent a new animal. Combine traits from different types of animals. Draw and color your animal. Then, answer the questions.

1. What is your new animal called?

_____

‑ ‑ ‑ ‑ ‑ ‑ ‑ ‑ ‑ ‑ ‑ ‑ ‑ ‑ ‑ ‑ ‑ ‑ ‑

_____

2. What animals does it have traits from?

_____

‑ ‑ ‑ ‑ ‑ ‑ ‑ ‑ ‑ ‑ ‑ ‑ ‑ ‑ ‑ ‑ ‑ ‑ ‑

_____

_____

‑ ‑ ‑ ‑ ‑ ‑ ‑ ‑ ‑ ‑ ‑ ‑ ‑ ‑ ‑ ‑ ‑ ‑ ‑

_____

Name: _____ Date: _____

Directions: Compare the parent and its offspring in the Venn diagram. Then, answer the question.

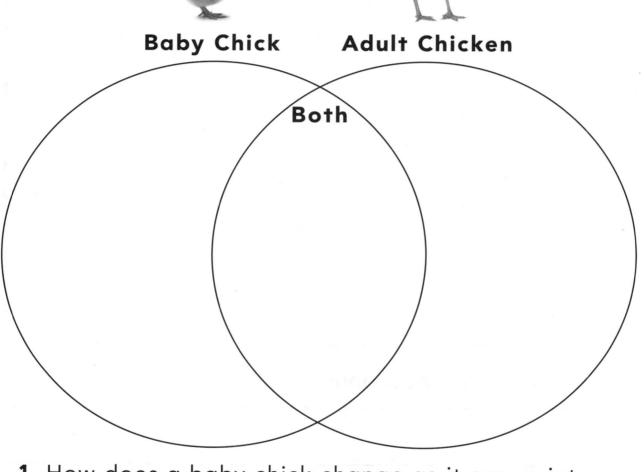

Baby Chick   **Adult Chicken**

Both

1. How does a baby chick change as it grows into an adult chicken?

_____

- -

_____

- -

_____

Name: _____ Date: _____

Directions: Read the text. Then, answer the question.

The Challenge

A toy store wants you to make some new toys. They want a set of three animal toys that are a family. They want the animals to be made-up. They can have any traits you want.

Criteria

- Your toy animal family must have parents. It must have an offspring.
- The offspring must have some traits from its parents.
- Your toy animals must stand on their own.
- Your toy animals must be made-up (do not really exist).

Constraints

- You may only use the materials you are given.
- The toy animals must be small enough to fit in your hand.

1. How do you feel about this challenge?

_____

_ _

_____

_ _

_____

Name: _____ Date: _____

Directions: Think about the animal traits you have learned about. Write ideas in the circles. Then, answer the question.

Animal Traits

1. What traits do you want your animals to have? (Examples: webbed feet, feathers, long neck)

_____

Parent A: _____

Parent B: _____

Offspring: _____

Name: _____ Date: _____

Directions: Sketch your animal family. Circle or label the traits that are similar.

Parent A

Parent B

Offspring

Name: _____ Date: _____

Directions: Write who will do each job. Add jobs if you need to. Then, make your animal toys. Check off the jobs as you complete them.

✔	To Do List	Student Name(s)
	Gather materials.	
	Build parent A.	
	Build parent B.	
	Build their offspring.	

Quick Tip!

It is okay to change jobs as you build. You can help others in your group. They can help you.

Name: _____ Date: _____

Directions: Place your three toy animals on a table. Watch to see if they stand on their own. Check the box next to each statement that is true. Then, answer the questions.

My toy animal family...	✓
has parents and one offspring.	
has an offspring with traits from its parents.	
is a type of animal I made up.	
can all stand on their own.	

1. What traits did the offspring get from its parents?

_____

_ _ _ _ _ _ _ _ _ _ _ _ _ _ _ _ _ _ _

_____

_ _ _ _ _ _ _ _ _ _ _ _ _ _ _ _ _ _ _

_____

2. How does the offspring look different from its parents?

_____

_ _ _ _ _ _ _ _ _ _ _ _ _ _ _ _ _ _ _

_____

_ _ _ _ _ _ _ _ _ _ _ _ _ _ _ _ _ _ _

Day 1

Name: _____ **Date:** _____

Directions: Think about your toy animal family. Answer the questions.

1. What do you like best about your animal toys?

_____

- -

_____

New Criterion Alert!

Make one more offspring. It should not look exactly the same as the first one.

2. How will the two offspring be the same?

_____

- -

_____

3. How will the two offspring be different?

_____

- -

_____

4. Write or draw ideas for what the new offspring could look like.

Name: _____ Date: _____

Directions: Sketch any changes you will make to your first three animal toys. Then, sketch the new offspring.

Original Animal Family

New Offspring

Name: _____ Date: _____

Directions: Rebuild your toy animal family. Make them better. Use this chart to help you.

✓	To Do List	Student Name(s)
	Gather new materials.	
	Change or rebuild parent A.	
	Change or rebuild parent B.	
	Change or rebuild first offspring.	
	Build a second offspring.	

Day 4

Name: _____ Date: _____

Directions: Place your toy animals on a table. Watch to see if they stand on their own. Check the box next to each statement that is true. Then, answer the questions.

My toy animal family...	✔
has parents and two offspring.	
has offspring with traits from their parents.	
has two offspring that are not exactly the same.	
is a type of animal I made up.	
can all stand on their own.	

1. What traits do the offspring share?

_____

_ _

_____

_ _

_____

2. How do the offspring look different?

_____

_ _

_____

_ _

_____

Day 5

Name: _____ Date: _____

Directions: Think about how you worked on this challenge. Draw kids playing with your toy animal family. Answer the question.

1. What do you call this new type of animal?

_____

– –

_____

🔘 **Talk About It!**

What could kids learn from playing with your animal family?

Conservation Teaching Support

Overview of Unit Activities

Students will learn about and explore natural resources and how to conserve them through the following activities:

- reading about and studying types of natural resources
- reading about and studying ways to conserve natural resources
- creating informational posters about conserving natural resources
- creating works of art from recycled materials
- analyzing a graph of ways students conserved resources
- creating reading forts out of old newspapers

Materials Per Group

Week 1

- basic school supplies
- poster board

- various recycled materials (egg cartons, cardboard tubes and boxes, packing material, old glue sticks, etc.)

STEAM Challenge

- basic school supplies
- glue
- newspapers (3+)

- stapler
- tape

Setup and Instructional Tips

- **Week 1 Day 4:** Ask students to bring recycled materials from home before this activity. Set expectations for how large or small student artwork may be.
- **STEAM Challenge:** The challenge can be done individually or in groups. If students are working in groups, have students sketch their own designs first. Then, have them share designs in groups and decide on one together.

Discussion Questions

- What are natural resources?
- What is conservation?
- How do humans harm Earth?
- How do humans help Earth?

- Which natural resource do you think is most important?
- Could we survive without natural resources? Why or why not?
- What things do we use that have been recycled?

Additional Notes

- **Possible Misconception:** Earth has an endless supply of natural resources.
  Truth: If resources are used too quickly, they could run out.

- **Possible Design Solutions:** Students may use rolled newspaper to make the structures of their forts. They might use flat newspaper to add roofs, walls, doors, or decorations.

Scaffolding and Extension Suggestions

- Support students by showing them examples of newspaper forts.

- Have students record how long they shower for a week. Challenge them to lower that amount the following week.

Answer Key

Week 1 Day 1
gold nugget—gold necklace
wheat field—loaf of bread
trees—wooden home frame
lake—glass of water

Week 1 Day 2
1. Recycle: soda can, newspaper, cardboard box
2. Trash: candy wrappers, banana peel

Week 1 Day 5
1. rode bikes
2. 8 students

Weeks 2 & 3
See STEAM Challenge Rubric on page 221.

Name: _____ Date: _____

Directions: Read the text. Draw lines to match the natural resources to how we use them.

All living things need natural resources to live. A natural resource is anything in nature we can use. Air and water are natural resources. Wood is a natural resource. We use it to build homes and other things. Plants are natural resources. We need them for food. Many of the things we use every day come from natural resources.

Natural Resource	**Human Use**

	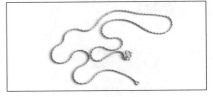

Talk About It!

What other natural resources can you think of?

Name: _____ Date: _____

Directions: Read the text. Label each item as *recycle* or *trash*.

Using natural resources must be done with care. We must conserve them. That means we must protect them. We can reduce how much we use. Take short showers to use less water. We can reuse things. Keep glass jars to store food in. We can recycle. Turn a plastic bottle into a piggy bank! Paper and aluminum can be recycled.

Recycle or Trash?

_____

- - - - - - - - - - - - - - - - - -

_____

- - - - - - - - - - - - - - - - - -

_____

- - - - - - - - - - - - - - - - - -

_____

- - - - - - - - - - - - - - - - - -

_____

- - - - - - - - - - - - - - - - - -

_____

Talk About It!

What are other ways you can reduce, reuse, or recycle?

Name: _____ Date: _____

Directions: Study the chart. Add your own ideas.
Make a poster all about the three Rs: reduce, reuse,
and recycle. Share ways to do them. Share why these
things are important.

Ways to Reduce	Things to Reuse	Things to Recycle
Take shorter showers.	clothes	plastic water bottles
Turn off lights.	books	soda cans
Walk or ride a bike instead of driving.	boxes	newspapers
Turn off water when you brush your teeth.	bags	cardboard

Name: _____ Date: _____

Directions: Make a piece of artwork with recycled materials. Answer the questions to plan your artwork. Then, make your work of art. Share it with others.

1. What materials will you use?

_____

_ _ _ _ _ _ _ _ _ _ _ _ _ _ _ _ _ _ _ _

_____

_____

_ _ _ _ _ _ _ _ _ _ _ _ _ _ _ _ _ _ _ _

_____

2. What do you want it to look like? Draw it.

Name: _____ Date: _____

Directions: Study the graph. Answer the questions.

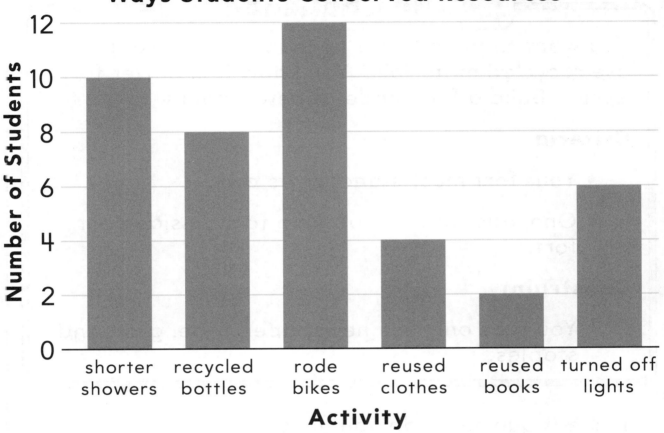

Ways Students Conserved Resources

1. Which activity was done by 12 students?

_____

– – – – – – – – – – – – – – – – –

_____

2. How many students recycled bottles?

_____

– – – – – – – – – – – – – – – – –

_____

3. Which of these activities could you do? Circle them on the graph.

Name: _____ Date: _____

Directions: Read the text. Then, answer the questions.

The Challenge

You want to build a fort to read in. You want to use recycled materials. You know it is better for Earth. Build a fort made of newspapers.

Criteria

- Your fort must stand on its own.

- One student must be able to sit inside your fort.

Constraint

- You may only use newspaper, tape, glue, and staples.

1. What questions do you have?

_____

— — — — — — — — — — — — — — — — — — — —

_____

— — — — — — — — — — — — — — — — — — — —

_____

2. How do you feel about this challenge right now?

not confident   **a little confident**   **very confident**

Day 2

Name: _____ Date: _____

Directions: Read the text. Study the pictures. Then, answer the questions.

Paper might not seem like good material to build with. But what happens when you roll it?

flat   **rolled**

1. Which style paper do you think is stronger?

rolled   **flat**

2. What parts of a fort could be made with rolled paper?

_____

- - - - - - - - - - - - - - - - - -

_____

3. What parts of a fort could be made with flat paper?

_____

- - - - - - - - - - - - - - - - - -

_____

 Talk About It!

What type of shape could your fort be?
Tell a friend about your ideas.

Name: _____ Date: _____

Directions: Sketch two fort designs. Try to make them very different. Then, choose your favorite.

Design 1

Design 2

Name: _____ Date: _____

Directions: Write who will do each job. Add jobs if you need to. Then, build your fort. Check off the jobs as you complete them.

✓	To Do List	Student Name(s)
	Gather materials.	
	Roll newspapers.	
	Staple parts together.	
	Tape or glue pieces or parts.	

 Quick Tip!

It is okay to change your design as you go!

Name: _____ Date: _____

Directions: Place your fort on the ground. Have one student sit inside of it. Answer the question.

Is your newspaper structure...	yes/no
made only of newspapers?	
connected with only tape, glue, and staples?	
able to stay up on its own?	
large enough to fit at least one student?	

1. Would you want to sit in your fort and read? Why or why not?

   _____

   _

   _____

   _ _ _ _ _ _ _ _ _ _ _ _ _ _ _ _ _

   _____

   _ _ _ _ _ _ _ _ _ _ _ _ _

   _____

Name: _____ Date: _____

Directions: Think about your fort design. Answer the questions. Plan how you will improve it.

1. What worked well in your fort design?

   _____

   _

   _____

2. What was hard about making your fort?

   _____

   _

   _____

3. Do you need to make your fort bigger?

   yes   **no**

4. Do you need to make your fort stronger?

   yes   **no**

New Criterion Alert!

Your fort must have decorations. They must be made of newspaper. Draw some ideas.

Name: _____ Date: _____

Directions: Sketch your new fort design. Circle the decorations you will add.

Name: _____ Date: _____

Directions: Rebuild your newspaper fort. Make it better. Use this chart to help you.

✓	To Do List	Student Name(s)
	Gather new materials.	
	Roll more newspapers.	
	Staple parts together.	
	Tape or glue pieces or parts.	
	Add decorations.	

Name: _____ Date: _____

Directions: Place your fort on the ground. Have one student sit inside of it. Answer the question.

Is your newspaper structure...	yes/no
made only of newspapers?	
connected with only tape, glue, and staples?	
able to stay up on its own?	
large enough to fit at least one student?	

1. What decorations did you add?

_____

- -

_____

_____

- -

_____

_____

- -

_____

Name: _____ Date: _____

Directions: Think about how you worked on this challenge. Draw a picture of yourself reading in your fort. Then, answer the question.

1. What was your favorite part about this challenge?

_____

_____

_____

_____

_____

 Talk About It!

Why might kids like to read in a fort?

The Moon Teaching Support

Overview of Unit Activities

Students will learn about and explore the moon through the following activities:

- reading about and studying a diagram of the moon's orbit
- reading about and studying pictures of the Apollo 11 mission
- making models of the phases of the moon with chocolate sandwich cookies
- making moon art with watercolors
- analyzing the phases of the moon
- creating straw rockets that launch to "the moon"

Materials Per Group

Week 1

- basic school supplies
- chocolate sandwich cookies (8)
- paper plate
- plastic spoon

- watercolors
- wax or white crayon
- white cardstock

STEAM Challenge

- basic school supplies
- cardstock
- construction paper
- cut-out picture of the moon (to aim rocket at)

- paper clip
- thin straw
- wide straw

Setup and Instructional Tips

- **Week 1 Day 3:** Set expectations for how students should handle the cookies (whether they may eat them and when).
- **STEAM Challenge:** This challenge is best done in partners or small groups. Have students sketch their own designs first. Then, have them share designs in groups and decide on one together.
- **Week 2 Day 1:** Attach a picture of the moon to a wall for students to aim at. Before students begin the challenge, show them where the moon is and where they will stand to launch their rockets.

Discussion Questions

- Why does the moon look different to us on different days?
- How does the moon give off light?
- How far away is the moon from Earth?
- Why do people want to explore the moon?
- Would you want to work for NASA? Why or why not?

Additional Notes

- **Possible Misconception:** The moon changes shape.
  Truth: The moon always stays a sphere. But at different times in the moon's orbit, we can only see the part that the sun's light is reflecting off of.
- **Possible Design Solutions:** Students may create rockets of different sizes. They may try different ways of launching their rockets, based on the examples given on Week 2 Day 2.

Scaffolding and Extension Suggestions

- Support students by showing them videos of people launching different types of straw rockets.
- Create a class calendar to chart the moon's phases over a month-long period.
- Have students research astronomers or moons of different planets and present their learning to the class.

Answer Key

Week 1 Day 1
1. B
2. C

Week 1 Day 2
1. Neil Armstrong
2. It was the first mission to land on the moon with people.

Week 1 Day 5
1. one
2. They are both lit about half. They are lit by the sun on the opposite side.

Weeks 2 & 3
See STEAM Challenge Rubric on page 221.

Name: _____ Date: _____

Directions: Read the text. Study the diagram. Then, answer the questions.

Earth has one moon. It does not always look the same. The moon orbits our planet. It moves in a curved path around Earth. It takes 28 days to go around Earth. The moon does not have its own light. We can see it because the sun shines on it. The light reflects off the moon.

moon

Earth

sun

orbit

1. The moon orbits _____ .

    (A) the sun   (C) a star

    (B) Earth   (D) itself

2. How long does it take the moon to orbit Earth?

    (A) 2 days   (C) 28 days

    (B) 8 days   (D) 280 days

Talk About It!

In your own words, describe what *orbit* means.

Name: _____ Date: _____

Directions: Read the text. Study the pictures. Then, answer the questions.

Apollo 11 was a special mission to the moon. It was the first one to land people on the moon. The people were a team. They worked together. Neil Armstrong was the leader of the team. It took them 76 hours to get to the moon. Armstrong was the first person to step onto the moon.

Apollo 11 launch

Neil Armstrong steps onto the moon.

_____

- - - - - - - - - - - - - - - -

1. _____ was the leader of the mission.

2. Why was *Apollo 11* a special mission?

_____

- - - - - - - - - - - - - - - -

_____

- - - - - - - - - - - - - - - -

_____

3. Would you travel to the moon? Why or why not? Tell a friend.

Name: _____ Date: _____

Directions: Follow the steps to make a model of the phases of the moon. Use the picture to help you.

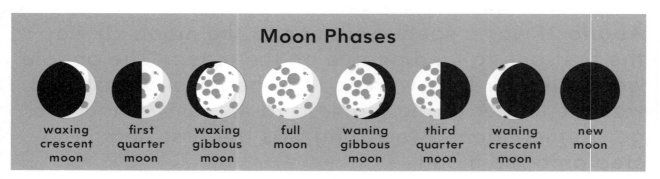

Moon Phases

waxing crescent moon | first quarter moon | waxing gibbous moon | full moon | waning gibbous moon | third quarter moon | waning crescent moon | new moon

1. Get one cookie for each phase.

2. Take off one side of each cookie. Set it aside.

3. Scrape the fillings with a spoon. Make them look like the moon in different phases.

4. Place the cookies on a paper plate. Put them in order.

5. Draw what your model looks like.

My Cookie Moon Phases

Name: _____ Date: _____

Directions: Follow the steps to create moon art.

1. Get a sheet of thick paper.

2. Use a white crayon to draw the moon. Draw circles all over your moon too. These will be moon craters.

3. Paint over your moon with watercolors.

4. When it is dry, draw a face on your moon. (*optional*)

5. Share your moon art with others. Teach them how to make it.

Try This!

Find out what a crater is. Learn about craters on the moon.

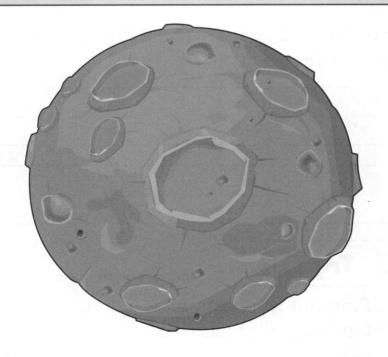

Day 5

Name: _____ Date: _____

Directions: Study the calendar. It shows the phases of the moon in one month. Then, answer the questions.

MON	TUE	WED	THU	FRI	SAT	SUN
						1
2	3	4	5	6	7	8
9	10	11	12	13	14	15
16	17	18	19	20	21	22
23	24	25	26	27	28	29
30	31					

_____

_ _ _ _

1. How many full moons are there in a month? _____

2. Compare the moons on the 12th and the 27th. Write what you notice.

_____

_ _ _ _ _ _ _ _ _ _ _ _ _ _ _ _ _ _ _

_____

_ _ _ _ _ _ _ _ _ _ _ _ _ _ _ _ _ _ _

_____

 Try This!

Find out when the next full moon is.
Go outside at night to look at it.

Name: _____ Date: _____

Directions: Read the text. Then, answer the questions.

The Challenge

NASA is looking for a new rocket engineer. You want them to choose you. You must show your skills. Make a straw rocket. Launch it to a moon on the wall.

Criteria

- Your rocket must launch by blowing air into a straw.

- Your rocket must reach a picture of a moon on a wall.

Constraint

- You may only use the materials you are given.

1. What question do you have?

_____

- - - - - - - - - - - - - - - - - - -

_____

_____

- - - - - - - - - - - - - - - - - - -

_____

2. What are you excited to try?

_____

- - - - - - - - - - - - - - - - - - -

_____

Name: _____ Date: _____

Directions: Read the text. Study the rocket launch ideas. Choose the one you want to try.

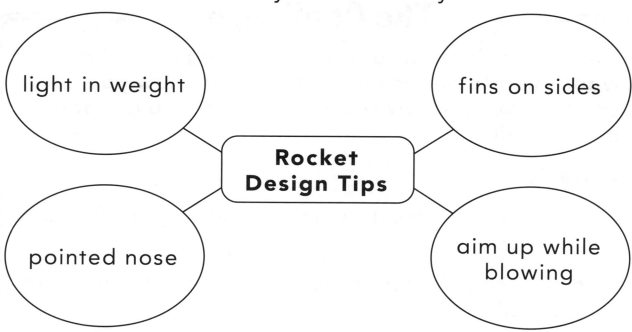

Rocket Launch Ideas

You must have a way to stick a straw in your rocket. There are different ways to do that. Here are some examples.

rolled paper   big straw and   paper pocket
                        little straw

Name: _____ Date: _____

Directions: Sketch your straw rocket design. Label the parts.

Rocket Parts

| nose | fins | straw |

Day 4

Name: _____ Date: _____

Directions: Write who will do each job. Add jobs if you need to. Then, build your straw rocket. Check off the jobs as you complete them.

✓	To Do List	Student Name(s)
	Gather materials.	
	Measure and cut materials.	
	Make the rocket shape.	
	Add fins.	
	Tape or glue parts.	
	Color and decorate your rocket.	

 Quick Tip!

If you are stuck, look at what others are doing. Get ideas from them! Ask for help.

Name: _____ Date: _____

Directions: Point your rocket toward the moon on the wall. Aim your rocket. Blow into your straw. Do a few more tests. Record the results.

> **Special Note for Teams:** All team members can test the rocket. Each person must use their own straw to launch it.

Launch Test	Did it hit the moon? (yes/no)	Notes About Flight Path
1		
2		
3		
4		

Day 1

Name: _____ Date: _____

Directions: Think about your straw rocket design. Answer the questions. Then, plan how you will improve it.

1. Did your rocket work the way you thought it would?

   yes   **no**

2. Do you need to change the way you launch your rocket?

   yes   **no**

3. Draw two rocket designs you saw from others on another sheet of paper. Tell a partner about the one that worked the best.

New Criterion Alert!

You can choose how you will improve your design. Draw a star next to one of these choices.

- I will make it bigger so it can hold more.

- I will make it go farther. I will stand farther away.

- I will add a paper clip to my rocket. This will show it can carry weight.

Name: _____ Date: _____

Directions: Sketch your new rocket design. Circle the parts that are new or different.

Unit 10: The Moon

Name: _____ Date: _____

Directions: Rebuild your straw rocket. Make it better. Use this chart to help you.

✓	To Do List	Student Name(s)
	Gather new materials.	
	Measure and cut materials.	
	Tape or glue parts.	
	Remove or change parts.	
	Add new parts.	
	Add or change decorations.	

Quick Tip!

You don't have to start from scratch. You can make changes to your first design.

Day 4

Name: _____ Date: _____

Directions: Point your rocket toward the moon on the wall. Aim your rocket. Blow into your straw. Do a few more tests. Record the results.

> **Special Note for Teams:** All team members can test the rocket. Each person must use their own straw to launch it.

Launch Test	Did it hit the moon? (yes/no)	Notes About Flight Path
1		
2		
3		
4		

Name: _____ Date: _____

Directions: Think about how you worked on this challenge. Draw yourself working on a part of this challenge. Then, draw yourself as a NASA engineer.

This Challenge

At NASA

 Talk About It!

What surprised you about this challenge?

The Seasons Teaching Support

Overview of Unit Activities

Students will learn about and explore how the seasons change through the following activities:

- reading about and studying the four seasons
- reading about and studying seasonal weather patterns
- drawing trees in different seasons
- drawing a silly creature dressed for one of the four seasons
- analyzing data of sunrises and sunsets
- creating bird baths

Materials Per Group

Week 1

- basic school supplies

STEAM Challenge

- basic school supplies
- cardboard tubes (4–6)
- clothespins (4–6)
- craft sticks (10+)
- plastic bowls (2)
- plastic cups (2 or more sizes; 2–4 of each size)

- plastic plates (2 or more sizes: 1–2 of each size)
- recycled jar lids (1–2)
- reusable plastic containers (optional)
- string (4–5 feet, 1.5 m)
- water ($\frac{1}{2}$ cup, 125 mL)
- wooden skewers (4–6)

Setup and Instructional Tips

- **STEAM Challenge:** The challenge can be done individually or in groups. If students are working in groups, have students sketch their own designs first. Then, have them share designs in groups and decide on one together.

Discussion Questions

- What is your favorite season? Why?
- Why do the seasons occur in the order they do?
- How do some animals prepare for winter?
- How do you know when spring is coming?
- What are some common winter activities?
- Why does it get warmer in spring and summer?
- How do the seasons affect people's lives?

Additional Notes

- **Possible Misconception:** Seasonal conditions are the same everywhere.
  Truth: Seasons are different depending on location. For example, some winter conditions can be very cold and snowy, while others may be mild.
- **Possible Design Solutions:** Students may make bird baths that hang on string. They may make ones that are supported by cups or craft sticks underneath.

Scaffolding and Extension Suggestions

- Support students by comparing temperatures and seasons in other countries as a group.
- Challenge students to make bird baths that can hold 1 cup (250 mL) or more of water.

Answer Key

Week 1 Day 1
The following items should be colored: flip flops, sun, sandcastle, sunscreen bottle, fan

Week 1 Day 2
Starting from top-left and moving clockwise: summer, fall, winter, spring

Week 1 Day 5
1. June
2. December; There was less sunlight.

Weeks 2 & 3
See STEAM Challenge Rubric on page 221.

Name: _____ Date: _____

Directions: Read the text. Color the pictures that relate to summer.

There are four seasons. They are summer, fall, winter, and spring. They happen in the same order each year. This is a pattern. Summer has the most hours of daylight. Earth gets more energy from the sun. That makes the air warmer.

It helps to know the patterns of the seasons. It helps us plan what to wear and do. It helps us plan where we want to go.

 **Talk About It!**

Name other things that are related to summer.

Name: _____ Date: _____

Directions: Read the text. Write the season under each picture. Then, answer the question.

Each season has typical weather patterns. Summer days are longer. The air gets hot. Winter is the coldest season. It snows in some places. Spring and fall have more mild temperatures. They are warm or cool. Many plants grow and bloom in spring. Many plants die or lose leaves in winter.

_____

_____

_____

_____

1. What is your favorite season? Tell a friend why.

Name: _____ Date: _____

Directions: Label each tree with a different season. Then, draw and color the tree to match the season. Add more details to each scene.

Name: _____ Date: _____

Directions: Choose a season. Then, draw a silly creature. Dress them so they are ready for the season! Show them doing an activity that goes with the season.

_____

— — — — — — — — — — — — — — — — — — — —

Season: _____

Name: _____ Date: _____

Directions: Study the sunrise and sunset data. Then, answer the questions.

Winter Sun

Date	Sunrise	Sunset	Daylight
December 18	6:50 am	4:45 pm	9 hours 54 minutes
December 19	6:51 am	4:45 pm	9 hours 53 minutes
December 20	6:52 am	4:45 pm	9 hours 52 minutes

Summer Sun

Date	Sunrise	Sunset	Daylight
June 6	5:40 am	8:00 pm	14 hours 20 minutes
June 7	5:40 am	8:01 pm	14 hours 21 minutes
June 8	5:40 am	8:02 pm	14 hours 22 minutes

1. Which month had more daylight?

December   **June**

2. Do you think it was cooler in June or December? Why?

_____

_ _ _ _ _ _ _ _ _ _ _ _ _ _ _ _ _

_____

_ _ _ _ _ _ _ _ _ _ _ _ _ _ _ _ _

_____

Name: _____ Date: _____

Directions: Read the text. Then, answer the question.

The Challenge

Spring is here! The sun is out, and it is warm. Birds need water to drink and to stay clean. Make a bird bath.

Criteria

- Your bird bath must be off the ground.

- Your bird bath must hold $\frac{1}{2}$ cup (125 mL) of water.

- Your bird bath must be decorated.

Constraint

- You may only use the materials you are given.

1. What are you wondering?

_____

_____

_____

_____

Name: _____ Date: _____

Directions: Your bird bath must be off the ground. Study the pictures to get ideas. Mark ideas you like.

Style 1	Style 2

Style 3	Style 4

Talk About It!

What other ideas do you have?

What materials will work best?

Name: _____ Date: _____

Directions: Sketch two bird bath designs. Try to make them very different. Choose your favorite.

Design 1

Design 2

Name: _____ Date: _____

Directions: Write who will do each job. Add jobs if you need to. Then, build your bird bath. Check off the jobs as you complete them.

✔	To Do List	Student Name(s)
	Gather materials.	
	Measure and cut materials.	
	Construct your bird bath.	
	Tape or glue parts.	
	Decorate the bird bath.	

Talk About It!

How close does your bird bath look to your design sketch? What is different?

Name: _____ Date: _____

Directions: Set up your bird bath. Hang it or place it on the ground. Pour $\frac{1}{2}$ cup (125 mL) of water in it. Answer the questions.

1. Is your bird bath off the ground?

   yes   **no**

2. How is it off the ground?

   it hangs   **it stands**

3. Did the water fit in the bird bath?

   yes   **no**

4. Did the water stay in the bird bath?

   yes   **no**

5. Write or draw to tell what decorations are on your bird bath.

Name: _____ Date: _____

Directions: Think about your bird bath design. Answer the questions.

1. My first bird bath (worked/did not work) because

_____

- - - - - - - - - - - - - - - - - - -

_____

- - - - - - - - - - - - - - - - - - -

_____

2. What do you want or need to change?

_____

- - - - - - - - - - - - - - - - - - -

_____

- - - - - - - - - - - - - - - - - - -

_____

3. What did you learn from making your bird bath?

_____

- - - - - - - - - - - - - - - - - - -

_____

- - - - - - - - - - - - - - - - - - -

_____

 Try This!

Did your first bird bath work great? Add a new part. Make a place to put bird food.

Name: _____ Date: _____

Directions: Sketch your new bird bath design. List any new materials you will need.

New Materials

_____   _____

- - - - - - - - - - - -   - - - - - - - - - - - -

_____   _____

- - - - - - - - - - - -   - - - - - - - - - - - -

_____   _____

Name: _____ Date: _____

Directions: Rebuild your bird bath. Make it better.
Use this chart to help you.

✓	To Do List	Student Name(s)
	Gather new materials.	
	Add or remove parts.	
	Tape or glue parts.	
	Check that parts are secure.	
	Decorate the bird bath.	

Name: _____ Date: _____

Directions: Set up your bird bath. Hang it or place it on the ground. Pour $\frac{1}{2}$ cup (125 mL) of water in it. Answer the questions.

1. Is your bird bath off the ground?

    yes   **no**

2. How is it off the ground?

    it hangs   **it stands**

3. Did the water fit in the bird bath?

    yes   **no**

4. Did the water stay in the bird bath?

    yes   **no**

5. My new bird bath design is better because

    _____

    _

    _____

    _

    _____

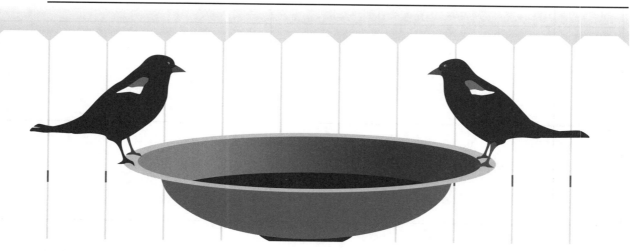

Name: _____ Date: _____

Directions: Think about how you worked on this challenge. Draw your bird bath in a garden. Show how birds will use it. Then, complete the sentence.

I think birds would use my bird bath because

_____

- -

_____

- -

☆ **Try This!**

Put your bird bath outside. See if birds come and use it!

The Stars Teaching Support

Overview of Unit Activities

Students will learn about and explore how stars and other objects move across the night sky through the following activities:

- reading about and studying stars
- reading about and studying patterns
- creating models of constellations
- drawing and naming new constellations
- analyzing data in a pictograph
- creating shoebox planetariums

Materials Per Group

Week 1

- basic school supplies
- small marshmallows (10–20)
- toothpicks (5–10)

STEAM Challenge

- basic school supplies
- blue and black construction paper (3–4 sheets)
- craft sticks (5+)
- foil
- glow-in-the-dark art materials (optional)
- pipe cleaners (5–10)
- shoebox
- string (2–3 feet, 1 m)
- white colored pencil
- white crayon

Setup and Instructional Tips

- **STEAM Challenge:** The challenge can be done individually or in groups. If students are working in groups, have students sketch their own designs first. Then, have them share designs in groups and decide on one together.

Discussion Questions

- What are patterns?
- What are patterns you notice in the night sky?
- Why can we see stars better in some places than others?
- What can we see in the sky during the day versus at night?

Additional Notes

- **Possible Misconception:** Stars stop shining during the day.
  Truth: Stars are always shining, even when we cannot see them.
- **Possible Design Solutions:** Students might place shoeboxes upside down to imitate dome-shaped structures. They might also set them up like dioramas. They might draw flat objects or glue and hang 3D objects.

Scaffolding and Extension Suggestions

- Create a list of the stars or constellations on chart paper, and display them for students to reference.
- Challenge students to research the legends or folktales behind different constellations.

Answer Key

Week 1 Day 1
1. A
2. C

Week 1 Day 2
1. moon
2. sun
3. star
4. constellation

Week 1 Day 5
1. Tyler
2. 4 shooting stars
3. Micah and Ana

Weeks 2 & 3
See STEAM Challenge Rubric on page 221.

Name: _____ Date: _____

Directions: Read the text. Study the picture. Then, answer the questions.

Stars are made of hot gases. They are very far away. Stars have their own light and heat. The sun is a star. It is the only star we see in the daytime. It is the closest star to Earth. That is why it looks so big and bright. There are stars that are bigger than the sun. But they are farther away. This makes them look smaller. We can only see other stars at nighttime. During the daytime, the sun is too bright. It blocks the light from other stars. The less city light there is at night, the more stars you can see.

1. Why does the sun look so big and bright?

(A) It is the closest star to Earth.

(B) It is the biggest star.

(C) It is the brightest star.

(D) It has the hottest gases.

2. Where would be the best time and place to look at stars?

(A) at night in a big city

(B) during the day in a big city

(C) at night in a desert

(D) during the day in the desert

Day 2

Name: _____ Date: _____

Directions: Read the text. Use the Word Bank to label the pictures.

A pattern is something that repeats. There are patterns you can see in the night sky. Stars appear to rise in one part of the sky and set in another part of the sky. The sun and moon appear to move in patterns too. Patterns are all around us in nature. A constellation is a group of stars. They make shapes that people notice.

Word Bank

| constellation | moon | star | sun |

1. _____

2. _____

3. _____

4. _____

Week
1

Day 3

Name: _____ Date: _____

Directions: Look at the constellations. Choose two to make models of. Make models with toothpicks and marshmallows.

Constellations

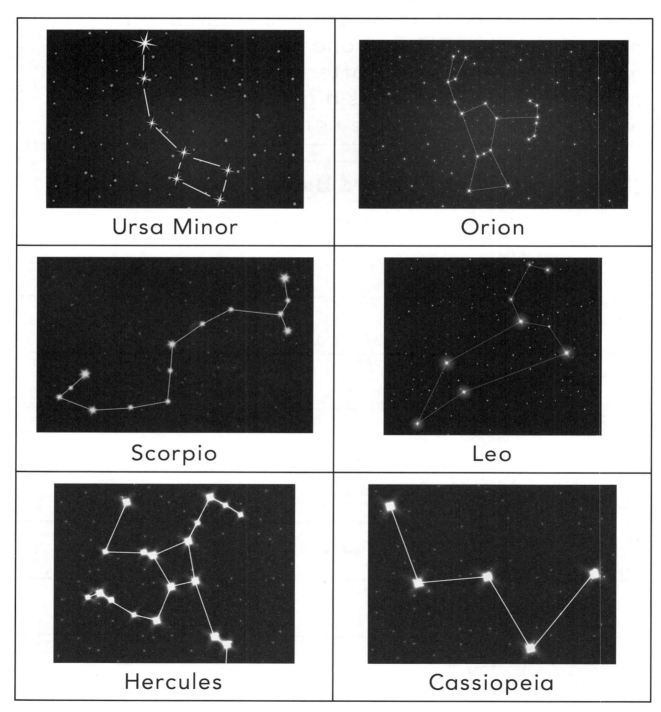

Ursa Minor

Orion

Scorpio

Leo

Hercules

Cassiopeia

Name: _____ Date: _____

Directions: Make your own constellation. Look for patterns in the stars. Draw lines between some stars to make a shape or picture. Complete the sentence.

1. The name of my constellation is

_____

_ _ _ _ _ _ _ _ _ _ _ _ _ _ _ _ _

_____.

Name: _____ Date: _____

Directions: Read the text. Study the pictograph. Then, answer the questions.

A few friends were looking for shooting stars. The graph shows how many each friend saw.

Shooting Star Sightings	
Micah	⭐ ⭐ ⭐
César	⭐
Emma	⭐ ⭐
Tyler	⭐ ⭐ ⭐ ⭐ ⭐
Ana	⭐ ⭐ ⭐

⭐ = 1 shooting star

1. Who saw the most shooting stars?

_____

_ _ _ _ _ _ _ _ _ _ _ _ _ _ _

_____

2. How many more shooting stars did Tyler see than César?

_____

_ _ _ _ _ _ _ _ _ _ _ _ _ _ _

_____

3. Which two friends saw the same number of shooting stars?

_____

_ _ _ _ _ _ _ _ _ _ _ _ _ _ _

_____

Name: _____ Date: _____

Directions: Read the text. Then, answer the question.

The Challenge

A planetarium is a special place. People go to them to see what the night sky looks like. Make a mini model of one that people can buy at the gift shop to take home. Make it in a shoebox.

Criteria

- Your planetarium must show a dark night sky.

- Your planetarium must show the moon and stars.

Constraint

- You may only use the materials you are given.

Look at the picture of a real planetarium. It is dark inside. This makes it look like night. It helps people see objects in the sky.

1. What do you notice?

_____

_ _ _ _ _ _ _ _ _ _ _ _ _ _

_____

_____

_ _ _ _ _ _ _ _ _ _ _ _ _ _

Name: _____ Date: _____

Directions: Think about what you might see in the night sky. Write ideas in the circles. Then, read the questions. Write or draw any ideas you have.

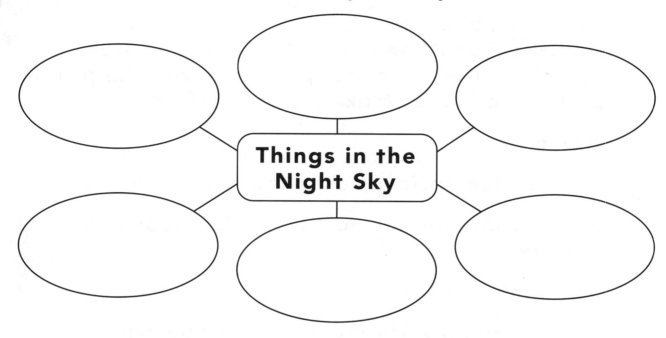

Things in the Night Sky

Things to Think About

1. How could you make it dark? What could you use to show the stars, moon, or other objects?

Name: _____ Date: _____

Directions: Sketch your shoebox planetarium. Label the parts.

Day 4

Name: _____ Date: _____

Directions: Write who will do each job. Add jobs if you need to. Then, build your shoebox planetarium. Check off the jobs as you complete them.

✓	To Do List	Student Name(s)
	Gather materials.	
	Create the dark sky in the entire shoebox.	
	Add stars.	
	Add a moon.	
	Add any other objects from your design.	

Talk About It!

Did you have any problems? What were they? How did you solve them?

Name: _____ Date: _____

Directions: Answer the questions about your design. Show your planetarium to others. Tell them about it. Write what they say.

Does your planetarium...	yes/no
have a dark night sky?	
have a moon?	
have stars?	
include ideas from all team members?	

Ask

1. What do you like about my design?

_____

- -

_____

- -

_____

2. How can I make it better?

_____

- -

_____

- -

_____

Name: _____ Date: _____

Directions: Think about your shoebox planetarium design. Answer the questions. Then, plan how you will improve your design.

1. What parts of your design work well?

   _____

   _

   _____

   _____

   _

   _____

2. Did it turn out how you planned?

   yes   **no**

3. What do you want or need to change?

   _____

   _

   _____

   _

   _____

   _____

   _

   _____

New Criterion Alert!

Add a constellation. If you already have one, add another! There are many. Draw and label it on another sheet of paper.

Name: _____ Date: _____

Directions: Sketch your new design. Circle the parts that are new or different.

Unit 12: The Stars

Name: _____ Date: _____

Directions: Rebuild your shoebox planetarium. Make it better. Use this chart to help you.

✔	To Do List	Student Name(s)
	Gather materials.	
	Darken the night sky, if needed.	
	Add more stars, if needed.	
	Add a constellation.	

Day 4

Name: _____ Date: _____

Directions: Answer the questions about your design.
Show your planetarium to others. Tell them about it.
Write what they say.

Does your planetarium...	yes/no
have a dark night sky?	
have a moon?	
have stars?	
have a constellation?	
include ideas from all team members?	

Ask

1. Do you like my new design better? Why or why not?

_____

- -

_____

- -

_____

2. How could it be better?

_____

- -

_____

- -

_____

Name: _____ Date: _____

Directions: Think about how you worked on this challenge. Draw yourself as an astronomer. Then, complete the sentences.

1. One thing I learned from this challenge was

_____

_ _ _ _ _ _ _ _ _ _ _ _ _ _ _ _ _ _ _

_____

_ _ _ _ _ _ _ _ _ _ _ _ _ _ _ _ _ _ _

_____

_ _ _ _ _ _ _ _ _ _ _ _ _ _ _ _ _ _ _

2. I am most proud of _____

_____

_ _ _ _ _ _ _ _ _ _ _ _ _ _ _ _ _ _ _

_____

Talk About It!

What else do you wonder about objects in space?

Name: _____ Date: _____

STEAM Challenge Rubric

Directions: Think about the challenge. Color in the faces to show what you did.

	Yes	A Little	Not Really
I used my materials appropriately.	😃	🙂	😐
I was creative. I had new ideas.	😃	🙂	😐
I worked well with others.	😃	🙂	😐
I followed directions.	😃	🙂	😐

Teacher Notes

_____

_____

_____

_____

Name: _____ Date: _____

Summative Assessment

Directions: Answer the questions.

1. What are two things engineers do?

_____

_ _ _ _ _ _ _ _ _ _ _ _ _ _ _ _ _ _ _

_____

_____

_ _ _ _ _ _ _ _ _ _ _ _ _ _ _ _ _ _ _

_____

2. You are building a dog house. Your material keeps breaking. What would you do? Tell why you made that choice.

Ⓐ make something different   Ⓒ ask a friend for help

Ⓑ look for different material

_____

_ _ _ _ _ _ _ _ _ _ _ _ _ _ _ _ _ _ _

_____

_____

_ _ _ _ _ _ _ _ _ _ _ _ _ _ _ _ _ _ _

_____

3. You want to make a new type of shoe. You look at other shoe designs. What would you do next? Tell a friend why you made that choice.

Ⓐ start making a shoe   Ⓑ start sketching a plan